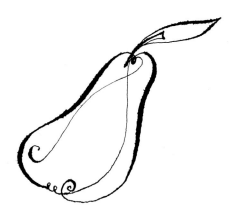

pears

BY LINDA WEST ECKHARDT

Photography by Karl Petzke

CHRONICLE BOOKS
SAN FRANCISCO

Karl Petzke would like to thank both Sue Fisher King and Fillamento
for the use of their beautiful things.

Library of Congress Cataloging-in-Publication Data:

Eckhardt, Linda West, 1939-
Pears / by Linda West Eckhardt : photography by Karl Petzke.
p. cm.
includes index.
ISBN 0-8118-0668-5
1. Cookery (Pears) 2. Pear. I. Title.
TX813.P43E35 1996
641.6'413—dc20   95-21505
                    CIP

Book and cover design: Gretchen Scoble
Lettering: Elvis Swift

Printed in Hong Kong.

Distributed in Canada by Raincoast Books,
8680 Cambie Street,
Vancouver, B.C. V6P 6M9

10 9 8 7 6 5 4 3 2 1

Chronicle Books
275 Fifth Street
San Francisco, CA 94103

CONTENTS

To Kaki, with love

INTRODUCTION

BEFORE OUR FAMILY MOVED to the Rogue Valley in Oregon, I thought pears were those things in a jar that babies liked best — certainly nothing that I'd be interested in. After all, I'd bought a few fresh ones in the grocery store from time to time and always found them to be hard and tasteless. What was all the commotion about pears?

But, as I say, that was before Oregon. After we'd moved to this pear-growing valley and summer had arrived, I was on one of my usual backroad sorties hunting for U-pick places when I ran across an orchard with a roadside stand. Never able to resist a bargain, I bought a forty-pound box of Bartletts, just picked that morning the farmer said, and get this: It cost less than five bucks.

Remember to let them ripen, he cautioned as he cut me off a slice of creamy pear, the juice running from his hand to my arm. Huh? I said, stupefied by the flavor and aroma of that perfect pear. But if you cut this one, aren't they all ripe? I asked.

He explained that the "tasters" had been picked two weeks before. Sure enough, I saw, lined up on a board, a row of bell-shaped Bartletts that did indeed look yellower than the ones in the box I'd just bought. Let 'em ripen up a few days, he went on.

I brought them home and set the box up on a kitchen stool. We walked around that box for about a week before the perfume in the kitchen overwhelmed us. Then the entire family simply fell on those pears. I ate nothing but pears for three or four days. My husband Joe and the three kids were a little more circumspect, but not much. We ate pears out of hand. Soon I was putting pears into cold summer soups. I made tarts. I made salsa. I made Joe's grandmama's pear pie with the flip-flop top — Lord! Did you ever see a grown man cry? We had a pearfectly fine summer that first year and all the twelve years since that we've lived in this pear-growing paradise. I've learned a lot about choosing, ripening, cooking, and putting up pears in the intervening years and want to share what I've learned with you.

In this book you'll find pear soups, side dishes, salads, condiments, sauces, main dishes, and finally, the category we always wait for: desserts, including several versions of the ubiquitous poached pears, tarts, pies, and cakes, as well as breads, muffins, and a focaccia. In addition, I'll also tell you how to choose and ripen pears and which varieties are best for what purpose.

I've tested recipes for three years to arrive at this collection. I've cooked with summer pears and winter pears. I've bought pears from the big three pear-growing states, Oregon, California, and Washington. I've worked with pears from south of the equator in the springtime when U.S. pears aren't always available. I've worked with dried pears and canned pears.

By the time you've cooked your way through this book, I hope you'll join me in saying that life can be pearfect, provided that you pick out good pears, let them ripen, and use an appropriate recipe. Happy cooking.

Linda West Eckhardt

BUT FIRST A LITTLE HISTORY

THE SENSUOUS PEAR has been a favorite fruit since prehistoric times. The Romans cultivated six varieties one hundred years before Christ and, by one hundred years after, they'd learned to graft trees and had developed more than forty varieties, which they cultivated throughout the Roman Empire.

Spanish missionaries brought the first pears to California, which remains one of the primary pear-growing areas in the country. To the pioneers, pears were as valuable as apples, not only for the fruit, but also for the wood, which was used in furniture making, and the leaves, which yielded a lovely yellow dye. One of our earliest hard liquor products was called perry, and was an alcoholic cider made from pears.

Ninety percent of America's pear crop is grown today in Washington, Oregon, and California. But pears are also grown in the Northeast and in parts of the Midwest. In addition, France, China, Japan, Turkey, Argentina, Chile, Austria, and South Africa also produce substantial pear crops.

HOW TO PICK
A PERFECT PEAR

UNRIPE *pears are rock hard, have no aroma, and range in color from green to tan.*

＊

UNDERRIPE *pears have begun to give off a slight perfume and color up, according to the variety, from green to yellow or bronze, but are still firm to the touch at the stem end.*

＊

RIPE *fruit will yield to gentle pressure at the stem end. The perfume of the pears should be overwhelming. The color will vary according to variety and range from yellow to bronze.*

＊

DEAD RIPE *pears are simply perfect: heavy with perfume, fully colored, and dripping with sweet juices.*

＊

OVERRIPE *pears are soft, with rotten cores and brownish bruises. They make great compost.*

PLANNING AHEAD is mandatory when thinking about pears, because they are picked mature but not ripe. Once you get the fruit home, it will be up to you to ripen it. You can do so by simply letting the fruit sit at room temperature. Slightly underripe, firm fruit is best for cooking, because it holds its shape, whether poached, baked, or braised. If the fruit you have is quite soft and mushy, it should be cooked into a sauce using sugar and a little lemon juice, but no water (see Chunky French Pear Sauce, page 101). This sugar-saturated cooking liquid will strengthen the structure of the ripe fruit so that it not only tastes great, but looks presentable as well. If you're in a hurry, place the fruit in a brown paper bag or a fruit-ripening bowl with a banana or a cut apple and close it so that the ethylene gas from the other fruit can speed up the ripening process.

Regardless of the variety of pear, choose fruit that is free of blemishes, bruises, or cuts. The fruit may be different colors, depending upon the variety, but it should be firm, smooth skinned, and have a slight perfume.

Once you have ripened the pears—either in a brown bag, a ripening bowl, or on the countertop of your warm kitchen—you may use the fruit or refrigerate it for 2 or 3 days.

Pears are held in cold storage at about 34°F. You can refrigerate them for a week or so, but don't expect the sugar conversion to work until you place them in a nice warm kitchen for at least 2 days.

PEAR VARIETIES

ANJOU: Named for the Anjou region of France, this large, thin-skinned yellowish green or red pear is available October through January. Although it can be mealy, it has a mild, delicate flavor and is excellent for cooking when still firm and underripe. When dead ripe, it's best for eating out of hand.

BARTLETT: A summer pear named for the New Englander who developed the variety, this pear is the one usually canned or made into purée, juice, or stewed pears. It's the classic pear shape, with a smooth yellow skin when ripe. Red Bartletts are also available. The perfume from the Bartlett will usually draw you from halfway across the room, and one bite into the sweet, succulent flesh explains why this is one of our favorite eating pears. The texture is fine, the flesh color is white to creamy, and this is the pear of choice for salads, for baking, and for braising.

BOSC: This gorgeous russet gold pear with a slender neck and long stem is available August through March. It's a firm-textured fruit, best used for cooking. This pear keeps well and is prized for its nutty vanilla flavor. I love to use it as a centerpiece in the fall, set on a bare walnut table with fiery fall leaves and walnuts.

CLAPP FAVORITE: An East Coast pear similar to the Bartlett, this first-of-summer pear is best eaten out of hand during its brief moment in the season.

COMICE: The Rolls-Royce of winter pears, this is the one you get in a box by mail order at Christmastime. Available from September to April, it's roundish in shape, with a medium yellow color when ripe, and a mild, buttery flavor. This fine-textured pear is best cut open and eaten with a spoon. This is the pear to serve with Brie or pecorino, or blue cheeses. It's terrific in fruit salads. Red Comice pears are also available. Underripe Comice pears are good for cooking and baking as well.

DEVOE: A green pear with a red blush, this New York state summer pear has an ivory flesh and an intense pear flavor. It is good for summer salads or for dessert.

FORELLE: Available October through February, this smallish pear with a freckled yellow skin develops rosy cheeks when ripe. It's an especially sweet and juicy pear that is fine for eating out of hand or for serving with cheese or in salads.

PACKHAM: Available from July through October, this cousin to the Bartlett looks like a summer Comice. It has a light green skin that turns yellow as it ripens. This fine-grained summer pear is good for eating out of hand or for cooking.

SECKEL: Miniature pears that are perfect for autumn and Christmas decorations, available from August to February, these smallish green to russet-colored pears with a pale yellow-white flesh are also ideal for canning, preserving, and pickling.

WINTER NELIS: Closest to Asian pears, these dense, firm-fleshed winter pears are available September through March and have a matte brown skin. These are what your grandmama called field pears, and they're best stewed or used in savory dishes.

Asian pears, now grown in California but originally from Japan, are a far-distant cousin to pears, being round and firm, and much more like an apple than a pear. It's really apples and oranges comparing pears and Asian pears, and they aren't recommended for substitution in pear recipes.

CoRing, PeELiNg, and CutTINg PEarS

It's easier to remove the core (seed pocket) from a whole pear before you peel it. Simply push the small end of a melon baller into the bottom of the pear and twist. After three turns you will have removed the entire core of the fruit. When you stand the fruit up, no one will be able to see where the core was. You can decide now whether to peel the fruit and remove the stem. To cook the whole fruit upright, cut a small slice off the bottom.

For halved fruit, you may cut the fruit in half lengthwise and cut out the stem end with a paring knife and remove the core with a melon baller or teaspoon.

For quartered, sliced, and chopped fruit, core the whole pear or first quarter it, then cut into the stem and core with a paring knife. Peel it and leave it in quarters, or cut it into wedges or slices, or chop as called for by the recipe.

If the core is discolored brown, soft, and mushy, the fruit is past its prime and probably should be pitched.

To peel pears after coring them, use a sharp paring knife or a sharp potato peeler. *Note:* Some recipes call for leaving the stem intact. After the fruit is peeled, drop it into a large bowl of water to which the juice of ½ lemon or 1 tablespoon of white vinegar has been added to prevent oxidation and discoloration of the pear. Drain the pears and pat them dry before using them in a recipe.

HOW TO USE THIS BOOK

I've taken a lot of grief over the years because I don't always use traditional cooking methods. Purists sometimes complain because I advocate using a microwave, as a tool in the cooking process. Do not despair if you don't have a microwave. A double boiler can be used in many cases, or a plain old pan on the stove in others. I've given you choices. But my real recommendation is that you put a microwave on your wish list. After all, they can be had for a hundred bucks or so. And since we've graduated to the stage where we realize that it's a tool — just like a good sharp knife — and not a panacea, it's my opinion that it is ridiculous not to use one.

Similarly, the food processor is the tool of choice for me for lots of procedures that are traditionally done using a balloon whisk or electric mixer. In recipes, I usually give the food processor method first. The second option may be a blender, an electric mixer, a whisk, or instructions for using your own two hands. The choice is yours. I do believe that, no matter what subject you tackle, the object of any cookbook is to teach you cooking technique. And part of becoming competent in the kitchen is knowing that you have options.

Now, as to measurements. I try always to give you measurements that are the easiest to follow. It drives me wild to see a recipe that calls for 12 cups of something, when it would be easier measured in 3 quarts. You don't have to have quart-measuring containers either. Just save those old spaghetti sauce quarts if that's your choice.

And as far as butter is concerned, I use unsalted butter rarely — when the flavor will be enhanced. That butter is more fragile and more expensive than others. So in most recipes, you'll just see the word *butter*.

I am fanatic about a few things. A melon baller makes handling pears so much easier. If you don't have one, get yourself to the store today and pick one up. If you just don't want to add this gadget to your kitchen stores, you can core pears with a grapefruit spoon or a teaspoon — but not nearly so neatly. Another handy tool is the fruit cutter. One downward motion and you've cored and sectioned pears or apples.

No matter how I plan to use a pear, I find it's simplest to hold the whole unpeeled pear in my left hand, and gouge through the bottom of the fruit with the small end of the melon baller. About three twists and the entire seed pod is gone. Then I can slice off the bottom so the pear will stand in a dish, I can peel it, I can quarter it, I can chop it. Whatever is called for, it's much simpler if you core the fruit before peeling it.

I always try to make a recipe as foolproof as possible. If you have any problems with a recipe, write me a letter and let me know. I'm not only always trying to develop and find better recipes, I'm always looking to teach technique and to improve my recipe-writing skills.

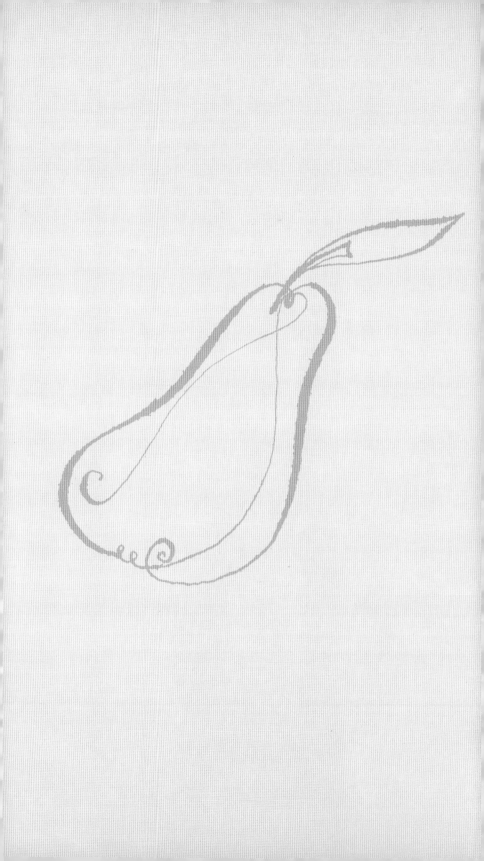

1.

Soups, Salads

and Appetizers

Queso Fresco Quesadillas with Pear Salsa

Pear and Chicken Bisque

Curried Butternut Soup with Diced Pear

Pear-Ginger Cream Soup

Oregon Spring Salad with Pears and Hazelnuts

Roasted Red Potato Salad with Bartlett Pears

Pear and Beet Salad with Watercress and Gorgonzola

Comice and Celery Root Salad

Pear and Tuna Salad with Walnuts and Bitter Greens

Pear and Pork Salad with Pine Nuts

Pear and Chicken Picnic Salad

QUESO FRESCO QUESADILLAS
WITH PEAR SALSA

*Nothing is quicker for entertaining than a quesadilla
made in a skillet. Cut it into pie wedges and serve hot. Made
with sweet pears and hot peppers, this oh-so-easy quesadilla
makes a stunning appetizer.*

MAKES 24 WEDGES

Pear Salsa

2 large unpeeled ripe Red Bartlett or
Comice pears, cored and cut into
thin slices

½ jalapeño chili, seeded and minced

2 tablespoons fresh lime juice

Grated zest of ½ lime

2 tablespoons minced fresh mint

½ teaspoon sugar

¼ teaspoon freshly ground black
pepper

3 tablespoons pine nuts, toasted
(see below)

1 cup (4 ounces) grated queso fresco
or crumbled goat cheese

Eight 9-inch flour tortillas

¼ cup (½ stick) unsalted butter

Whole fresh mint leaves for garnish

TO MAKE THE SALSA: Combine all the ingredients in a small bowl. Toss to mix. Cover and set aside.

ASSEMBLE THE QUESADILLAS by sprinkling each of 4 tortillas with about ¼ cup cheese, then top each with 3 to 4 tablespoons salsa. Top with the remaining tortillas. Cook them, one at a time, in a hot skillet filmed with butter over medium heat for about 3 to 5 minutes on each side, or until the cheese is melted and the tortillas are browned. Cool them slightly on a cutting board, then cut each one into 6 wedges. Garnish with mint leaves and serve.

TOASTING PINE NUTS

Shake pine nuts in a hot skillet until browned, about 30 seconds, or bake them in a preheated 350°F oven until browned, about 3 minutes. Take care not to burn them. They leap from browned to burned in an instant.

PEAR AND CHICKEN BISQUE

*Pears yield a subtle perfume to this soup served cold in
summer or warm in winter. Think of this as year-round comfort food.*

MAKES 6 SERVINGS

1 whole chicken breast (8 ounces)

1½ quarts (6 cups) cold water

2 tablespoons butter

4 russet potatoes (about 2 pounds),
    peeled and diced

4 large ripe pears (Bartletts,
    Packhams, Boscs, or Anjous),
    cored, peeled, and diced

2 shallots

¼ teaspoon of sugar

Juice of ½ lemon

Salt, freshly ground black pepper, and
    cayenne pepper to taste

½ cup heavy (whipping) cream

Chopped fresh chives for garnish

PLACE CHICKEN BREAST and water in a medium-large soup pot and simmer for 30 minutes.

REMOVE THE CHICKEN BREAST from the broth. Discard the skin and bones and shred the meat. Cover the meat and set it aside. Pour the broth into a bowl and place it in the freezer.

IN THE SAME POT, melt the butter over medium-high heat and sauté the potatoes, pears, and shallots, sprinkling the mixture with sugar, for about 10 to 15 minutes, or until the color begins to turn golden. Add the lemon juice and season with salt, pepper, and cayenne pepper.

DISCARD THE FAT from the chicken broth. Add about 1 quart (4 cups) of broth to the pot, reduce the heat, cover, and simmer for about 15 minutes, or until the vegetables and fruits are tender. Purée with the cream in a food processor fitted with the steel blade or in a blender. Return the mixture to the pot, reheat, adding the shredded chicken. Season with salt and pepper. Serve in soup bowls, sprinkled with chives.

CURRIED BUTTERNUT SOUP
WITH DICED PEAR

*The sweetness of pear
counterbalances the curry in this heavenly chilled soup.
Serve as a first course or a fine spring lunch.*

MAKES 4 SERVINGS

1½ pounds butternut squash
1 teaspoon butter
1 large yellow onion, sliced
4 garlic cloves
¼ teaspoon sugar
2 teaspoons curry powder
Salt and freshly ground black pepper
    to taste
3 cups low-fat chicken broth
1 cup (8 ounces) nonfat plain yogurt
1 large ripe Winter Nelis, Bosc,
    Anjou, or Comice pear
8 fresh mint leaves for garnish

PRICK THE SQUASH with a fork in several places. Cook the squash whole for about 40 minutes in a 350°F oven, or microwave on High (100 percent power) for 10 minutes. Let it rest 10 minutes. Cut the squash in half and scoop out and discard the seeds, then scoop the flesh into a bowl.

MELT THE BUTTER in a soup pot over medium heat, then add the onion and stir. Cover and cook the onion until tender, about 5 to 8 minutes. Add the garlic and sugar, remove the lid, increase the heat to medium high, and cook and stir for 2 minutes, or until the onion begins to brown.

SPRINKLE IN THE CURRY powder and season with salt and pepper. Cook and stir for 1 minute, then add the cooked butternut squash. Cook for 2 to 3 minutes, then pour in the broth. Bring to a boil, reduce the heat, and simmer for about 10 minutes. Purée the soup in a food processor fitted with the steel blade or in a blender, then cover and refrigerate.

WHEN THE SOUP IS thoroughly chilled, stir in all but 1 tablespoon or so of the yogurt. Peel, core, and cut the pear into fine dice, then stir it into the soup. Divide the soup among 4 soup bowls, garnishing it with mint leaves and a jot of the remaining yogurt.

PEAR-GINGER CREAM SOUP

*Smooth, subtle, perfumed—here's a pear soup that will
intoxicate your guests. Follow it with a simple entrée. Float an edible
flower, such as a nasturtium or a pansy, in the soup for maximum effect.
The recipe may be halved for smaller parties.*

MAKES TEN 1-CUP SERVINGS

1 tablespoon butter

1 onion, finely chopped

3 pounds underripe pears of the
season, cored, peeled, and
chopped (about 6 cups)

⅛ teaspoon ground cinnamon

2 quarts (8 cups) homemade or
canned low-salt chicken broth

2 teaspoons coarsely chopped fresh
ginger

½ cup heavy (whipping) cream

Garnish

3 tablespoons crystallized ginger,
chopped

3 tablespoons minced fresh chives

Edible flowers such as pansies or
nasturtiums (optional)

MELT THE BUTTER over low heat in a heavy soup pot, then add the onion and cook for 5 minutes, or until the onion becomes translucent. Add the chopped pears. Cook, uncovered, until the pears are tender, about 10 minutes. Stir in the cinnamon, chicken broth, and fresh ginger. Bring to a boil, then reduce to a simmer and cook for 20 minutes.

WITH A SLOTTED SPOON, lift out the solids and transfer them to a food processor fitted with the steel blade or a blender. Process to a smooth purée, then return the purée to the soup. Stir in the cream and heat through.

TO SERVE, spoon the soup into individual bowls and top with crystallized ginger and chives. Float an edible flower in the soup if you wish. Serve at once.

OREGON SPRING SALAD WITH PEARS AND HAZELNUTS

In mixed baby greens, or mesclun, *pale and dark green, bronze, and red leaves, smooth and ruffled shapes, sweet and tart tastes are combined. With ripe Comice or Packham pears, goat cheese, and hazelnuts, you'll have everything at once: sweet, salty, sour, bitter, and smooth.*

MAKES 4 SERVINGS

DIVIDE THE BABY GREENS among 4 dinner plates. Top with the cabbage, then the cheese and nuts. Fan the pear slices on top.

4 cups (4 ounces) mixed baby greens

1 cup finely shredded red cabbage

3 ounces goat or feta cheese, crumbled (about ¾ cup)

2 tablespoons hazelnuts or walnuts, toasted (see note, following) and chopped

1 large ripe Comice or Packham pear, cored, peeled, and sliced thin

Raspberry-Mustard Vinaigrette

¼ cup olive oil

2 tablespoons raspberry vinegar

2 teaspoons Dijon mustard

⅛ teaspoon salt

Freshly ground black pepper to taste

MAKE THE VINAIGRETTE by shaking all the ingredients together. Drizzle this over the salad and serve at once.

NOTE: To toast and peel nuts, toast the hazelnuts in a preheated 325°F oven for 3 to 7 minutes, or until just beginning to brown. Or, place in a microwave oven on High (100 percent power) for 2 minutes. Stir the nuts once in the middle of toasting, and take care that you don't let them burn.

FOLD THE HAZELNUTS in a hot towel and roll the nuts around inside the towel, then pick them out of the skins. Chop the nuts on a cutting board or by barely pulsing them in a food processor fitted with the steel blade or in a blender.

ROASTED RED POTATO SALAD
WITH BARTLETT PEARS

The addition of just-ripe Bartletts to a roasted red potato
salad makes a potluck winner. By roasting potatoes on a rock salt bed
instead of the more ordinary boiling, you'll get a crisp punched-up flavor
in the potatoes before you ever begin the salad.

MAKES 8 SERVINGS

2 pounds small red potatoes

1 cup rock salt (for baking the
potatoes)

¼ cup unseasoned rice vinegar

1 teaspoon sugar

1 teaspoon Dijon mustard

1 tablespoon Madras curry powder

Salt and freshly ground black pepper
to taste

½ cup fruity olive oil

3 green onions with tops, sliced on the
diagonal

¼ cup chutney

3 large ripe Bartlett pears, cored,
peeled, and quartered

1 head butter lettuce

¼ cup chopped pistachio nuts for
garnish

PREHEAT THE OVEN to 375°F.
Arrange the rock salt on a large baking
sheet with sides. Place the potatoes in
one layer on the salt, then bake until
tender, about 15 to 20 minutes. Remove the potatoes from the rock salt
bed and let cool.

PLACE THE VINEGAR, sugar, mustard, curry powder, salt, and pepper in
a small jar with a lid. Shake vigorously
until the mixture is thick and smooth.
Pour the oil in, then shake again until
the mixture is thoroughly blended.
Stir in the green onions and chutney.

SLICE THE POTATOES into a large
bowl. Add the quartered pears. Coat
the potatoes and pears with the dress-
ing, tossing gently. Salt and pepper to
taste.

TO SERVE, line a shallow bowl with
lettuce leaves and spoon in the potato-
pear mixture. Top with pistachio nuts.

PEAR AND BEET SALAD WITH
WATERCRESS AND GORGONZOLA

*Keep baby beets in a jar, and you can make this salad
the moment your pears are perfectly ripe. Colorful, sweet, salty,
bitter, and sour, it's good winter or summer.*

MAKES 4 SERVINGS

2 cups stemmed watercress (1 large
  bunch)
2 large ripe Comice or Bartlett pears,
  cored, peeled, and sliced thin
One 14-ounce jar whole baby beets,
  drained
½ cup (2 ounces) crumbled
  Gorgonzola
½ cup fresh raspberries
¼ cup hazelnuts, toasted, peeled, and
  finely chopped (see page 28)

Raspberry Vinaigrette
¼ cup raspberry vinegar
½ cup extra-virgin olive oil
½ teaspoon salt
Freshly ground black pepper to taste

TO COMPOSE THE SALAD: Divide
the watercress among 4 dinner plates.
Add fanned pear slices, 3 baby beets,
and Gorgonzola to each plate. Top
with the raspberries and hazelnuts.

WHISK TOGETHER the vinaigrette,
then drizzle over the salad and serve
immediately.

COMICE AND CELERY ROOT SALAD

*Winter salad with the crunch of celery root
and the sweetness of the season's sweetest pear makes a fine
side dish for pork or poultry meals.*

MAKES 4 SERVINGS

2 large ripe Comice pears, cored,
    peeled, and chopped
2 cups finely shredded peeled celery
    root
¼ cup white wine vinegar
2 teaspoons packed brown sugar
½ teaspoon salt
Freshly ground black pepper to taste
¼ cup vegetable oil
8 red leaf lettuce leaves
2 tablespoons fresh lemon juice

COMBINE THE PEARS and celery root in a large bowl. In a small bowl, whisk together the vinegar, brown sugar, salt, and pepper, then whisk in the oil. Pour over the pears and celery root. Cover and refrigerate for 1 hour or longer.

TO SERVE, divide the lettuce leaves among 4 dinner plates. Top with pear and celery root salad. Grind additional fresh black pepper over and sprinkle with fresh lemon juice.

PEAR AND TUNA SALAD
WITH WALNUTS AND BITTER GREENS

*Take your lunchtime tuna salad uptown with the
addition of ripe pears, crunchy walnuts, and bitter greens. Add hot
French bread and cold Chardonnay, and it's lunch.*

MAKES 2 SERVINGS

2 large ripe Anjou or Comice pears,
    cored, peeled, and chopped
½ cup chopped celery
⅔ cup chopped walnuts
2 teaspoons fresh lemon juice
One 7½-ounce can water-packed
    tuna, drained
2 tablespoons light mayonnaise
2 cups (2 ounces) bitter greens
    (escarole, spinach, romaine, or
    mixed baby greens)

COMBINE THE PEARS, celery, walnuts, and lemon juice and toss in a medium bowl. Add the tuna and mayonnaise and toss to mix. Serve on a bed of bitter greens.

PEAR AND PORK SALAD
WITH PINE NUTS

*Here's autumn on a plate. Serve
alongside a loaf of hot French bread and a bottle of robust
red wine for a fine end-of-season picnic.*

MAKES 4 SERVINGS

1 pound pork tenderloin

1 garlic clove, minced

1 tablespoon minced fresh ginger

1 tablespoon soy sauce

¼ cup sake

½ teaspoon sugar

½ teaspoon dark sesame oil

4 cups (4 ounces) mixed baby greens

2 large ripe Comice pears, cored,
    peeled, and cut into wedges

Vinaigrette

2 tablespoons extra-virgin olive oil

2 teaspoons balsamic vinegar

1 teaspoon soy sauce

½ teaspoon dark sesame oil

½ teaspoon sugar

Salt and freshly ground black pepper
    to taste

½ teaspoon grated fresh ginger

1 tablespoon pine nuts

PREHEAT THE OVEN to 450°F.
Place the pork loin in a glass baking
dish. Rub the meat with the garlic and
ginger. Roast the meat until it reaches
an internal temperature of 160°F,
about 20 to 30 minutes. Remove from
the oven and let it cool. While the
meat is cooling, mix together the soy,
sake, sugar, and sesame oil. Pour this
mixture over the meat and let it marinate at room temperature for at least
1 hour. Cut the meat into thin slices.
TO SERVE, divide the baby greens
among 4 dinner plates. Fan slices of
pork on the greens, then add the pear
wedges. Stir together the vinaigrette
and pour it over the pork and pears.
Sprinkle pine nuts over all.

PEAR AND CHICKEN PICNIC SALAD

*Make the chicken-pear mixture and refrigerate
until serving time, then simply arrange it on top of cold greens.*

MAKES 4 SERVINGS

¼ cup extra-virgin olive oil

2 whole chicken breasts, boned,
    skinned, and cut into 1½-inch
    strips (about 1 pound total)

½ cup walnut halves

½ teaspoon salt

Freshly ground black pepper to taste

3 tablespoons minced shallots

2 tablespoons white wine vinegar

2 large ripe Bartlett pears, cored,
    peeled, and thinly sliced

8 cups (8 ounces) mixed baby greens

HEAT 2 TABLESPOONS of the oil in a large skillet over medium-high heat then add the chicken and walnuts. Sauté until the chicken is cooked through, about 5 minutes. Remove to a large bowl and season with salt and pepper. Cover and set aside.

ADD THE SHALLOTS to the skillet and cook over medium heat until translucent, about 2 minutes. Add the vinegar and bring to a boil, stirring to scrape up the brown bits from the bottom of the skillet. Remove from heat and whisk in the remaining 2 tablespoons oil. Add the pears, stir gently to coat them, then add this mixture to the chicken mixture. Cover and refrigerate.

TO SERVE, divide the baby greens among 4 dinner plates and top with the chicken-pear mixture.

2.
Main Dishes

Savory Pear Bread Pudding

Peppered Pear and Cheddar Bread Pudding

Malaysian Gingered Fish with Pears

Balsamic Pear-Salmon Sauté

Seared Scallops and Pears with Lemon-Vodka Sauce

Chicken and Pear Teriyaki

Baked Chicken with Tarragon, Mustard, and Winter Pear

Duck with Christmas Pears

Pork Chop, Chipotle, and Pear Sauté

Stir-fried Sirloin and Pears on a Bed of Spinach

SAVORY PEAR BREAD PUDDING

*This dish is great for company because you
make it one day before serving. It's fabulous for Sunday brunch.
The smooth custard is both hot and sweet.*

MAKES 8 SERVINGS

8 ounces stale French bread, cut into
¾-inch-thick slices (about 4
cups)

2 large eggs

3 cups low-fat (1 percent) milk

½ teaspoon salt

½ teaspoon freshly ground black
pepper

⅛ teaspoon cayenne pepper

2 tablespoons sugar

4 large ripe Bosc or Winter Nelis
pears, peeled, cored, and halved

½ cup fresh mint leaves

¼ cup grated Parmesan cheese

THE DAY BEFORE you plan to serve
this dish, coat a 9-by-13-inch baking
dish with vegetable-oil cooking spray.
Arrange 1 layer of bread slices on the
bottom of the dish, fitting them tightly
into the bottom of the pan.

WHISK TOGETHER THE EGGS,
milk, salt, pepper, cayenne, and sugar
in a medium bowl. Pour this mixture
over the bread, cover with plastic
wrap, and refrigerate overnight.
About 1 hour before serving time,
remove the dish from the refrigerator.

PREHEAT THE OVEN to 350°F.
Arrange the pears evenly over the top
of the soaked bread so that you can
make 8 square servings once the
pudding is baked.

CHOP HALF OF THE MINT and
strew it over the pears and custard.
Sprinkle the Parmesan evenly over the
entire dish. Bake, uncovered, for 45
minutes, or until lightly browned.

REMOVE THE PUDDING from the
oven and let it stand for about 15 minutes. Cut the pudding into 8 squares,
tuck the remaining whole mint leaves
around the pears, and serve at once.

PEPPERED PEAR AND CHEDDAR BREAD PUDDING

For Easter brunch, this makes a perfect centerpiece.
Put the pudding together an hour before your celebration begins, or the
night before. The pepper adds zest to the sweet pears, and each square
explodes with flavor. Serve with bacon and mimosas.

MAKES 8 SERVINGS

1 cup fresh bread crumbs

5 tablespoons butter at room temperature

8 cups ⅝-inch-thick ripe Bosc or Winter Nelis pear slices (about 8 pears — 4 pounds — cored and peeled)

2 tablespoons packed brown sugar

1⅛ teaspoons salt

¼ teaspoon ground cinnamon

2¼ teaspoons cracked peppercorns

Zest of 1 lemon, julienned

2 tablespoons fresh lemon juice

Sixteen ¾-inch-thick day-old slices French or country bread

3 cups half-and-half

½ cup polenta (coarse cornmeal)

4 large eggs

1 teaspoon Dijon mustard

2 cups (8 ounces) shredded sharp white Cheddar

COAT A DEEP 3-QUART baking dish with vegetable-oil spray, sprinkle with bread crumbs and set aside.

MELT 2 TABLESPOONS of the butter in a 12-inch skillet over medium heat and add the pears. Cook uncovered until the pears begin to brown, then sprinkle with the brown sugar and ⅛ teaspoon of the salt. Raise the heat to medium high and cook until the sugar begins to caramelize, about 2 minutes. Sprinkle the pears with cinnamon and ¼ teaspoon of the cracked pepper. Add the lemon zest and juice and boil, stirring, until it evaporates, about 3 minutes. Set aside and let cool until barely warm.

BUTTER THE BREAD SLICES with the remaining butter, then cut them into 1-inch squares; set aside. In a medium saucepan over medium heat, bring the half-and-half to a simmer, then sprinkle in the polenta and cook for 3 minutes, stirring. Remove from heat. Whisk the eggs, mustard, and the remaining 1 teaspoon salt in a medium bowl.

(continued)

Spoon a little of the hot cream mixture into the eggs, whisk, then pour all the egg-cream mixture into the hot cream and whisk vigorously.

ARRANGE ONE THIRD of the bread pieces in the baking dish. Sprinkle with 1 teaspoon of the cracked pepper, half the cheese, and half the pears. Repeat with another third of the bread, more pepper, and the remaining cheese and pears. Top with the remaining bread. Carefully pour the hot cream mixture over, allowing the liquid to flow down the sides. Cover and refrigerate for 30 minutes to overnight.

TO BAKE, preheat the oven to 350°F. Place a large roasting pan one-quarter full of hot water on the middle shelf of the oven. Remove the cover from the baking dish and place the dish in the water bath. Bake the pudding until the top is a rich golden brown, the middle is puffed, and a knife inserted in the center comes out clean, about 1 hour. Let cool on a rack for 20 minutes and serve.

MALAYSIAN GINGERED FISH
WITH PEARS

*Whole steamed fish
on a bed of rice makes a meal in itself.*

MAKES 2 SERVINGS

2 pan-sized trout or grouper (about 1
   pound total)
2 large ripe Bartlett pears, cored,
   quartered, and peeled

Ginger Sauce
2 tablespoons dry white wine
2 tablespoons low-salt soy sauce
½ teaspoon dark sesame oil
1 teaspoon Asian chili-garlic paste
1 tablespoon unseasoned rice vinegar
½ teaspoon sugar
3 green onions with tops, smashed and
   slivered
3 quarter-sized pieces fresh ginger, cut
   into matchsticks
4 garlic cloves, minced
1 tablespoon minced lemongrass
   (optional)

2 cups steamed rice (see page 122)
½ cup chopped fresh cilantro leaves
   for garnish
½ lime, cut into wedges, for garnish

PLACE THE FISH AND PEARS in a
glass pie plate. Combine all the ginger
sauce ingredients in a small bowl and
stir to mix thoroughly. Pour the mixture over the fish. In a wok or deep
pot, bring about 2 inches of water to
a boil. Put the pie plate of fish on a
steamer tray or trivet, cover, reduce
heat, and steam the fish over simmering water until the fish flakes easily,
about 20 minutes.

SERVE THE FISH AND PEARS on a
bed of rice, napped with the sauce
from the bottom of the pie plate. Garnish with cilantro and wedges of lime.

BALSAMIC PEAR-SALMON SAUTÉ

*A one-pan dish that simply sings. Accompany
with wild-and-brown-rice pilaf, then tuck in a few sprigs of
flat-leaf parsley for a celebration dinner that's ready in less than
30 minutes. This recipe is easily doubled or tripled.*

MAKES 2 SERVINGS

2 salmon steaks, about 4 ounces each

¼ teaspoon salt

½ teaspoon freshly ground black
    pepper

1 teaspoon unsalted butter

4 shallots, sliced thin

1 garlic clove, sliced thin

2 large ripe Bartlett, Bosc, or Winter
    Nelis pears, cored, peeled, and
    halved

¼ teaspoon whole fennel seed

¼ cup pear eau-de-vie (pear brandy)

¼ cup balsamic vinegar

Fresh flat-leaf parsley sprigs for
    garnish

PAT THE STEAKS dry with a paper towel, then season with salt and pepper. Set aside. Preheat a large nonstick skillet over medium-high heat. Coat the skillet with butter and heat until the butter foams, then add the steaks. Arrange the shallots and garlic around the steaks. Add the pear halves, cut-side down, around the steaks. Cook for about 5 minutes, or until the steaks are brown on one side, then turn. Sprinkle the fennel seed over everything.

MIX THE EAU-DE-VIE and vinegar in a cup, then pour over the steaks. Cook for about 3 to 5 minutes longer, or until the steaks are done, the pears are tender, and the liquid has reduced to a thick dark syrup.

SERVE EACH DINNER PLATE with a salmon steak, 2 pear halves, and a topping of the shallot-garlic balsamic syrup. Garnish with a generous amount of flat-leaf parsley.

SEARED SCALLOPS AND PEARS WITH LEMON-VODKA SAUCE

If you want to impress just one person with an absolutely divine dinner, this is a perfect choice. Serve the dish on a brightly colored plate, uncork a bottle of wine, toss a salad, offer a loaf of crusty hot bread— and enjoy a four-star dinner.

MAKES 2 SERVINGS

2 tablespoons olive oil

2 teaspoons unsalted butter

8 ounces large sea scallops

2 large ripe Bartlett, Anjou, or Bosc pears, cored, peeled, and halved

8 ounces fresh fettuccine, or 4 ounces dried fettuccine

Lemon-Vodka Sauce

Grated zest and juice of 1 lemon

½ cup heavy (whipping) cream

2 tablespoons vodka

1 tablespoon chopped fresh chives

Salt and freshly ground black pepper to taste

3-inch pieces fresh chives for garnish

Julienned lemon zest for garnish

HEAT 1 TABLESPOON of the oil and 1 teaspoon of the butter in a 10-inch skillet over medium heat until the butter foams, then sauté the scallops for about 2 to 3 minutes per side, or until golden, turning once. Transfer to a warmed plate, cover, set aside, and keep warm.

WIPE OUT THE PAN with a paper towel, add the remaining 1 tablespoon oil and 1 teaspoon butter, and heat over medium-high heat until the butter foams. Place the pears in the pan, cut-side down, and sauté until golden, 2 or 3 minutes, then turn and cook the rounded side until golden. Remove from heat and keep warm.

AT THE SAME TIME, fill a 4-quart pot with salted water and bring it to a full boil. Drop the fettuccine into the boiling water and cook for about 2 minutes for fresh and 8 minutes for dried, or until al dente. Drain.

MAKE THE SAUCE: Mix the lemon zest and juice and set aside. Combine the cream and vodka in a small saucepan and boil for 3 minutes. Add the chives and mixed juice and zest, and boil for 1 minute, or until thickened.

TOSS THE HOT PASTA with the sauce. Divide between 2 warmed dinner plates. Top with seared scallops and season with salt and pepper. Arrange 2 pear halves on either side of the scallops on each plate. Garnish with chive pieces and lemon zest and serve at once.

CHICKEN AND PEAR TERIYAKI

*Quick to fix, sweet, and saucy, this makes a fine
midweek dinner when served on a bed of couscous. Add a
tossed green salad and a bottle of Chardonnay.*

MAKES 4 SERVINGS

2 tablespoons butter

2 cups (about ½ pound) small brown
mushrooms, thinly sliced

½ cup finely chopped onion

2 large underripe Bartlett pears,
cored, peeled, and halved

4 boneless, skinless chicken breast
halves (about 4 ounces each),
pounded to an even thickness

Salt and freshly ground black pepper
to taste

¼ cup teriyaki sauce

¼ cup water

2 tablespoons orange marmalade

Couscous (see page 122)

MELT THE BUTTER in a 10-inch skillet over medium-high heat and sauté the mushrooms and onion until the onion begins to brown, about 5 minutes. Add the pear halves, cut-side down, to the pan. Sauté, turning several times, until the pears begin to brown, about 3 to 5 minutes. Push the fruit and vegetables to the sides of the skillet and place the chicken breasts in the pan. Season with salt and pepper. Stir together the teriyaki sauce, water, and marmalade. Pour the mixture over the chicken. Cover and cook, turning from time to time, until the chicken is golden brown, about 20 minutes.

TO SERVE, make a bed of couscous on each plate, then top with a chicken breast, some mushrooms and onion, and a pear half. Serve hot.

BAKED CHICKEN WITH TARRAGON, MUSTARD, AND WINTER PEAR

*The bitter bite of mustard, the subtle licorice
hint of tarragon, cayenne's heat, and the luscious sweet flavor
of winter pear complement baked chicken breasts.*

MAKES 2 SERVINGS

1 tablespoon unsalted butter

½ teaspoon cayenne pepper

1 tablespoon minced fresh tarragon,
   or 1 teaspoon dried tarragon

1 teaspoon balsamic vinegar

2 tablespoons Dijon mustard

Salt and freshly ground pepper to taste

Two 4-ounce boneless, skinless
   chicken breast halves

1 large ripe winter Bosc or Anjou pear,
   cored, peeled, and cut into 8
   sections

Couscous (see page 122) for serving

PREHEAT THE OVEN to 375°F. Melt the butter in a large ovenproof skillet. Stir the cayenne, tarragon, balsamic vinegar, mustard, salt, and pepper into the butter. Dredge the chicken pieces in this mixture. Arrange the pear sections around the chicken.

BAKE THE CHICKEN, uncovered, for 15 to 20 minutes, or until the skin is a rich, golden brown and the juices run clear when the chicken is pierced with a knife.

SERVE with couscous.

DUCK WITH CHRISTMAS PEARS

The rich flavor of duck enhances the sweet tartness of fruit.
Here in the Rogue Valley, we have an abundance of glorious winter pears
to cook with come Christmas. Serve with wild rice pilaf and
a side of cranberry relish.

MAKES 6 SERVINGS

3 wild or 2 domestic ducks, plucked, cleaned, rinsed, and dried (6 to 7 pounds total)
2 tablespoons olive oil
Salt, cayenne pepper, and freshly ground black and white pepper to taste
3 large underripe Comice, Bosc, or Anjou pears
2 cups dry white wine, plus more as needed
2 tablespoons honey
¼ cup minced fresh ginger
2 tablespoons cornstarch
½ cup brandy

Christmas Pears
6 ripe Comice, Bosc, or Anjou pears
3 tablespoons unsalted butter
3 tablespoons honey
½ cup orange juice
Juice and grated zest of ½ lemon

PRICK THE DUCKS all over with a fork so that fat can run out. Heat the oil in a large Dutch oven over medium heat and brown the ducks on all sides. Spoon the fat out of the pan and discard. Season the ducks lightly with salt and generously with cayenne and white and black pepper.

WHILE THE DUCKS are browning, core, peel, and chop the 3 pears. In a food processor fitted with the steel blade or in a blender, purée the pears with the 2 cups wine, the honey, and ginger. Add this sauce to the ducks. Bring to a boil, then reduce heat, cover, and simmer until the ducks are tender, spooning the sauce over them from time to time and adding wine as needed to keep at least 2 inches of liquid in the pan at all times. Domestic ducks will be tender in about 1 hour. Wild ducks, who had to work for a living, will probably take 2 hours to become completely fork tender.

WHILE THE DUCKS are cooking, prepare the Christmas pears: Core and peel the pears, then cut them in half lengthwise. To microwave, place the pears in a buttered microwavable baking dish. In a small microwavable bowl or measuring cup, combine the butter, honey, orange juice, lemon juice, and zest. Bring to a boil in the microwave on High (100 percent power), then pour the liquid over the pears. Cover tightly with plastic microwave wrap and microwave on High (100 percent power) until tender, about 6 minutes. Alternatively, poach covered in a large saucepan on the stove until tender, about 12 minutes. Let the pears stand, then pour their juice into the duck cooking pot.

WHEN THE DUCKS are cooked and the pears are ready, get out a big platter. Arrange the ducks and pears on it. Cover loosely with aluminum foil and place in a warm oven while you prepare the sauce.

RAISE THE HEAT under the Dutch oven to high and cook the sauce to reduce it by at least half. Dissolve the cornstarch in the brandy and stir the mixture into the sauce. Cook and stir for several minutes until the sauce is thick. Taste and adjust the seasoning with salt, cayenne, and pepper. Pour a little sauce over the birds and serve the rest in a gravy boat.

Pork Chop, Chipotle, and Pear Sauté

*Sweet pears and hot chipotle chilies complement pork loin chops.
This makes a fine dinner served with couscous or rice. In winter, use
Bosc pears and garnish with kumquats. In summer, try Bartletts.*

MAKES 4 SERVINGS

4 boneless pork loin chops (about
    1 pound), fat trimmed

Marinade
2 dried chipotle chilies, minced
3 tablespoons low-salt soy sauce
3 tablespoons dry sherry
¼ cup orange juice
3 tablespoons water
1 tablespoon dark sesame oil
1½ tablespoons honey
2 garlic cloves, pressed
½ teaspoon grated fresh ginger
2 large underripe Bartlett or Bosc
    pears, cored, peeled, and halved
Couscous or rice for serving
    (see page 122)

PLACE THE PORK CHOPS in a glass dish. To make the marinade: Combine all of the ingredients in a small jar. Shake well and pour the mixture over the chops. Cover and refrigerate for 4 hours to overnight.

ABOUT 45 MINUTES BEFORE serving time, preheat a large nonstick skillet over medium-high heat. Lift the chops out of the marinade with a slotted spatula and sauté them in the hot pan, spooning the reserved marinade over them 1 tablespoon at a time and turning them occasionally until they're a dark mahogany color. After about 15 minutes, add the pears and spoon the marinade over them as well. Cook and turn the pears until they're golden, about 10 minutes. Serve the pork chops and pears on a bed of couscous or rice.

STIR-FRIED SIRLOIN AND PEARS ON A BED OF SPINACH

*The rich flavor of beef works admirably with that of sweet pears
and spinach. Marinate the steak and pears in an Asian-scented sauce.
If you use packaged prewashed spinach, dinner is done in 45 minutes,
and that includes 30 minutes to marinate the beef.*

MAKES 4 SERVINGS

Marinade

¼ cup hoisin sauce

2 tablespoons low-salt soy sauce

1 tablespoon water

2 teaspoons dark sesame oil

4 garlic cloves, crushed

1 tablespoon unseasoned rice wine
vinegar

¼ teaspoon red pepper flakes

3 tablespoons minced fresh cilantro

3 large, underripe winter pears such
as Bosc or Comice, cored,
peeled, and cut into ⅛-inch strips

1 pound boneless top sirloin, 1 inch
thick, cut into ⅛-inch strips

2 teaspoons vegetable oil

10 ounces fresh spinach, stemmed and
washed

¼ cup sliced green onions with tops

1 tablespoon water

½ cup fresh cilantro leaves for garnish

1 tablespoon sesame seeds, toasted,
for garnish

Steamed rice for serving (see page
122)

STIR THE MARINADE ingredients together in a medium bowl. Pour half the marinade into a second bowl. Place the pears in one and turn them to coat. Place the beef strips in the other bowl. Rub the marinade into the beef strips with your fingers. Cover both bowls and set aside for at least 30 minutes.

DRAIN THE BEEF and discard the marinade. Preheat a wok or large non-stick skillet over high heat. Add 1 tea-spoon of the oil. Stir-fry the beef for 1 to 2 minutes, or until the outside is no longer pink. With a slotted spoon, transfer to a warm platter. Add the pears to the pan and stir-fry until they begin to brown, about 2 minutes, then transfer them to a bowl. Heat the re-maining 1 teaspoon oil in the pan, then add the spinach and green onions. Toss until the spinach is wilted, about 30 seconds. Add the water to the pan, cover, and steam 30 seconds.

MAKE A BED of the spinach mixture on a warmed serving platter and top with the pears, then the warm beef. Garnish with cilantro leaves and sesame seeds and serve.

3.

Side Dishes

PEAR AND SPINACH PURÉE

GERMAN-STYLE PEARS AND CABBAGE

SWEET POTATO FRITTERS WITH PEAR COULIS

PEAR-SOY SAUTÉ

PEAR AND SPINACH PURÉE

Heavenly with ham and hot biscuits, this surprising
side dish elevates a down-home dinner to company fare. The spinach
color won't reveal your secret until the lucky diners take the first bite
of this sublime dish that blends two dissimilar foods.

MAKES 6 SERVINGS

2 pounds spinach, stemmed

2 large dead-ripe Comice or Bartlett
    pears, cored, peeled, and
    quartered

2 tablespoons unsalted butter

2 tablespoons half-and-half

Salt and freshly grated nutmeg to taste

½ small ripe Comice or Bartlett pear,
    cored, peeled, and cut into a fan
    shape with stem intact, for
    garnish

FILL A 4-QUART SOUP POT with
water and bring to a rolling boil. Drop
all the spinach in by the handful and
stand and watch the pot. Yes, it will
boil, at which moment you should in-
stantly dump the spinach into a colander and run cold water over it until it's
cool. Use your hands to squeeze out
all the excess water. Place the spinach
and pears in a food processor fitted
with the steel blade or in a blender and
purée.

MELT THE BUTTER in a 12-inch
skillet until it foams, then add the
spinach purée. Cook and stir until it
begins to boil, then add the half-and-
half and season with salt and nutmeg.

SERVE IN A CUT CRYSTAL bowl,
swirling the top. Garnish with the
fanned pear half.

GERMAN-STYLE PEARS AND CABBAGE

Great with pork chops and mashed potatoes,
this hot salad was one of my grandmama's favorites.

MAKES 6 SERVINGS

8 cups shredded red cabbage (about
    1 pound)

5 medium underripe pears (about
    2½ pounds), cored, peeled, and
    sliced (5 cups)

4 cups boiling salted water

4 bacon slices, diced

1 medium yellow onion, sliced (about
    1 cup)

2 tablespoons balsamic vinegar

2 tablespoons sugar

1 teaspoon fennel seed, crushed
    (optional)

Freshly ground pepper to taste

IN A LARGE SAUCEPAN, simmer the cabbage and pears in the water for about 5 minutes, or until barely tender; drain and place in a large bowl.

AT THE SAME TIME, in a medium skillet, stir the bacon and onion over medium heat for about 5 minutes, or until the onion is tender and the bacon is cooked. Stir in the vinegar, sugar and (optional) fennel seed. Pour over the cabbage and pears and toss to mix lightly. Sprinkle with pepper and serve.

SWEET POTATO FRITTERS
WITH PEAR COULIS

*Luscious pumpkin-colored pancakes are served alongside
a sweet pear coulis. Remember, always use a stainless steel knife
and grater when cutting a sweet potato. Using a carbon blade will
cause the sweet potato to darken.*

MAKES 6 SERVINGS

1 pound sweet potatoes, peeled and
    coarsely shredded

3 large eggs

¼ cup chopped green onions

3 tablespoons all-purpose flour

½ teaspoon salt

¼ teaspoon ground mace

¼ cup vegetable oil

Pear Coulis (see pg 122)

WRAP THE SWEET POTATOES in a clean dish towel and wring to remove the excess moisture. Combine the shredded sweet potatoes and all the remaining ingredients except the oil and coulis in a medium bowl; blend well.

HEAT THE OIL in large nonstick skillet over medium-high heat. Spoon 1 heaping tablespoonful of batter into the skillet, flattening the mixture with the back of a spoon.

COOK UNTIL GOLDEN on one side, then turn over and brown the second side, for a total cooking time of about 4 minutes. Transfer with a slotted spoon to paper towels to drain. Keep warm in the oven while you finish cooking the remaining batter. Serve with the pear coulis alongside.

PEAR-SOY SAUTÉ

As an accompaniment to grilled pork or chicken,
this Bartlett pear side dish is a good addition to a summer dinner.

MAKES 4 SERVINGS

¼ cup (½ stick) butter
3 tablespoons low-salt soy sauce
1 tablespoon grated fresh ginger
½ cup packed brown sugar
¼ teaspoon cayenne pepper
4 medium Bartlett pears, cored,
    peeled, and halved
2 tablespoons unseasoned rice vinegar

MELT THE BUTTER in a large skillet, then stir in the soy, ginger, brown sugar, and cayenne and stir to dissolve the sugar. Add the pear halves, cut-side down. Reduce heat and simmer, uncovered, until the pears are tender, about 10 minutes. Using a slotted spoon, lift the pears onto a serving platter. Stir the vinegar into the sauce, raise heat, and boil until the sauce is thick and syrupy. Pour the sauce over the pears and serve.

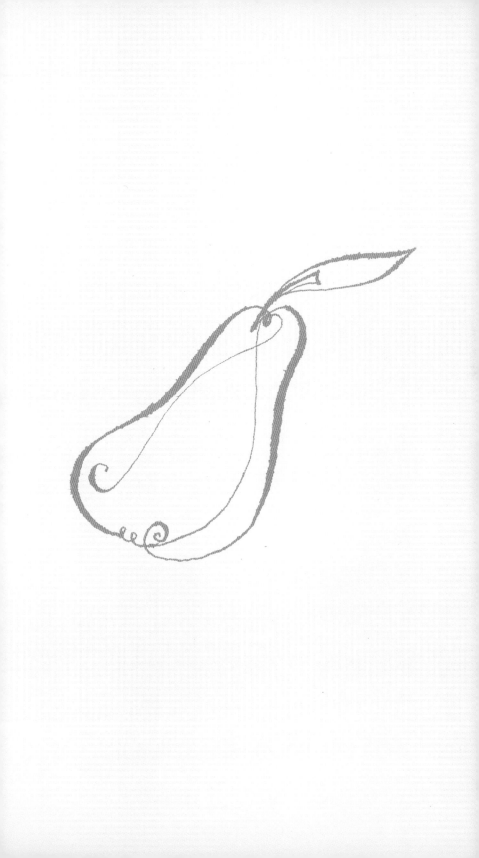

4.
Condiments and Preserves

PEAR CAPONATA

FRESH AND DRIED PEAR PRESERVES

GREEN TOMATO, APPLE, AND PEAR MINCEMEAT

PRESERVED SECKELS WITH LEMON

SECKEL PEAR SALSA IN PEAR SHELLS

SUE NAUMES'S PEAR HARLEQUIN

SPICY PRESERVED PEAR CHUTNEY

PEAR CAPONATA

Spread this mellow relish on toasted baguette or country bread slices. Serve as a first course with a glass of robust red wine.

MAKES 4 CUPS

1 eggplant, sliced thick

¼ cup extra-virgin olive oil

Salt to taste

2 teaspoons sugar

2 ripe Bartlett, Comice, or Bosc pears

1 large onion, chopped

4 garlic cloves, minced

2 cups chopped Roma (plum) tomatoes, juice reserved, or one 28-ounce can Italian tomatoes, drained and chopped, juice reserved

2 tablespoons capers, drained

¼ cup currants

1 tablespoon balsamic vinegar

½ teaspoon freshly ground black pepper

2 tablespoons pine nuts, toasted (see page 22), for garnish

PREHEAT the oven to 425°F. Coat 2 baking sheets with vegetable-oil cooking spray.

USING 2 TABLESPOONS of the oil, brush both sides of the eggplant slices and arrange them on one of the baking sheets. Sprinkle the eggplant lightly with salt and 1 teaspoon of the sugar. Roast for 25 minutes, or until the eggplant is tender and brown, turning the slices over when they are half done.

WHILE THE EGGPLANT is roasting, core and peel the pears, cut them into chunks, and spread them on the second baking sheet. Brush them with 1 tablespoon of oil and sprinkle on the remaining sugar. Bake for about 25 minutes, or until golden brown, shaking the baking tray from time to time.

HEAT THE REMAINING tablespoon olive oil in a large skillet over medium heat and sauté the onion and garlic until golden, about 7 to 10 minutes. When the eggplant is cooked, add it, together with the chopped tomatoes and their juice and the capers, and

(continued)

simmer over medium-low heat for about 10 minutes, stirring occasionally.

ADD THE COOKED PEARS and currants to the eggplant mixture and season with vinegar and salt and pepper. Cook for 5 to 10 minutes. Transfer to a serving bowl, sprinkle with pine nuts, and serve warm or at room temperature.

FReSH AND DrIed PeaR PReSeRveS

Mixing fresh and dried pears with eau-de-vie
(pear brandy) yields a textured product with an intense pear
perfume. Spoon a little of this onto your morning toast or over a dish
of vanilla ice cream. It's tart, sweet, and rich.

MAKES 1 PINT

8 ounces dried pears, chopped

8 large Bartlett pears, cored, peeled, and cut into small pieces

Julienned zest and juice of 2 or 3 lemons (about ½ cup juice)

1 tablespoon grated fresh ginger

½ cup maple syrup

2 tablespoons pear eau-de-vie (pear brandy)

COMBINE THE DRIED and fresh pears in a heavy, medium-large saucepan. Stir in the zest, juice, ginger, and maple syrup. Cook over medium heat, stirring from time to time, until the mixture is as thick as jam, about 20 minutes. Stir in the eau-de-vie. Transfer to a hot sterilized pint jar, seal with a hot sterilized lid, and let cool. This will keep in the refrigerator for about 3 weeks.

GREEN TOMATO, APPLE, AND PEAR MINCEMEAT

If you can use a food processor, chop the tomatoes, apples, and pears separately. Pulse so as not to purée them. To make a pie, pour 1 pint of mincemeat into an unbaked 9-inch pie shell and bake in a preheated 350°F oven for 35 minutes. Serve with whipped cream.

MAKES 8 PINTS

3 pounds completely green tomatoes, coarsely chopped (about 6 medium tomatoes)

1 tablespoon noniodized salt

3 pounds (about 6) green Granny Smith or Pippin apples, cored, peeled, and coarsely chopped

3 pounds pears (about 6), underripe Bartlett or Anjou, cored, peeled, and coarsely chopped

2 cups (12 ounces) golden raisins

Grated zest, juice, and chopped pulp of 2 oranges

Grated zest of 2 lemons

½ cup unseasoned rice vinegar

½ cup frozen apple juice concentrate

3 ½ cups packed dark brown sugar

2 teaspoons ground cinnamon

½ teaspoon ground allspice

½ teaspoon ground cloves

½ teaspoon ground ginger

½ cup dark Jamaican rum

½ cup (1 stick) butter, melted

COMBINE THE CHOPPED green tomatoes with the salt, stir, and pour into a colander to drain for 1 hour.

COMBINE THE DRAINED tomatoes with all the remaining ingredients except the rum and butter in a large stainless steel pot. Bring to a boil over medium heat, then lower the temperature and simmer until thick, about 1 hour. Stir from time to time to keep the mixture from sticking to the bottom.

STIR IN THE RUM, then ladle the mincemeat into 8 hot sterilized pint canning jars, leaving a ¾-inch headspace. Spoon 1 tablespoon of melted butter atop each jar, then seal with hot sterilized canning lids.

PROCESS in a boiling-water bath for 25 minutes (see page 73). Let cool, label, and store the jars in a cool, dark place. The mincemeat will keep for up to 1 year. It is best if you let it mellow for at least 1 month before using.

NOTE: For making the pie, pour 1 pint of filling into an unbaked 9-inch pie shell and bake in a preheated 350°F oven for 35 minutes. Serve with whipped cream.

PRESERVED SECKELS WITH LEMON

The sweet little Seckel makes an ideal
canning pear. Bartletts may be substituted with good results.

MAKES 6 PINTS

6 pounds underripe Seckel pears
(about 12 medium pears)
Juice of ½ lemon in a large bowl of
water
5 cups water
2 cups sugar
Six ½-by-3-inch lemon zest strips
Juice of 1 lemon
6 whole cloves
6 pieces (about 2 tablespoons)
crystallized ginger
One 1-inch piece cinnamon stick,
broken into 6 pieces

HALVE, CORE, AND PEEL the
pears. Drop the pears into the lemon
water as you work. Combine the 5
cups water, sugar, lemon zest and juice
in a large stockpot. Bring the mixture
to a hard boil and stir to dissolve the
sugar. Reduce heat to a simmer, then
add the pears. Cook the pears until
tender, about 5 to 10 minutes.

DIVIDE THE PEARS and syrup
among 6 hot sterilized pint jars, leaving ½ inch headspace at the top of
each jar. Add 1 clove and 1 piece each
of ginger and cinnamon to each jar.
Seal with hot sterilized lids and
process in a boiling-water bath for 20
minutes (see page 73). Store in a cool,
dark place.

SECKEL PEAR SALSA IN
PEAR SHELLS

*Sweet little Seckels marry well with fresh cranberries
and a touch of fresh jalapeño. These salsa-filled pear halves make
a fine garnish for roast turkey or baked ham.*

MAKES 4 SERVINGS

1 cup fresh cranberries
½ jalapeño chili, seeded
¼ cup sugar
4 Seckel pears, cored and halved
1 teaspoon white wine vinegar

CHOP THE CRANBERRIES, jalapeño, and sugar by pulsing in a food processor fitted with the steel blade or in a blender. Transfer to a small bowl, cover, and refrigerate for 1 hour.

TO SERVE, scoop the pear flesh out of each half, leaving a ¼-inch shell. Chop the pear flesh coarsely, then toss it with the cranberry mixture. Sprinkle the vinegar over and mix. Fill the pear shells with the mixture and arrange them around a roast turkey or baked ham.

SUE NAUMES'S
PEAR HARLEQUIN

Sue Naumes is one of the West's premier pear orchardists.
She gave me the pear corer I use when canning. This old-fashioned
condiment, my grandma's favorite sauce, looks like a jewel
and is great over homemade ice cream.

MAKES 8 QUARTS

3 large oranges

6 pounds underripe Anjou, Seckel, or
  Bartlett pears (about 12 medium
  pears)

Juice of ½ lemon in a large bowl of
  water

One 16-ounce can crushed pineapple,
  drained

Grated zest and juice of 2 lemons

1 cup maraschino cherries, drained

1 cup (4 ounces) walnut halves

CUT OFF THE ORANGE ZEST in very fine strips with a zester or a vegetable peeler and place the zest in a small saucepan. Add water to cover and simmer over medium-low heat until the zest is tender, about 5 minutes. Drain. Meanwhile, seed the oranges, dice the orange flesh and set it aside.

CORE, PEEL, AND SLICE the pears, dropping them into the lemon-scented water to prevent darkening. Drain the pears and combine them with the pineapple and blended orange zest. Cover and let stand 12 hours or overnight. Drain the juice into a large nonaluminum pot and boil it for 20 minutes.

ADD THE FRUIT, lemon juice, and zest. Cook and stir for 20 minutes, or until the fruit begins to look translucent. Add the cherries and nuts and cook for 5 minutes. Pack the fruit into hot sterilized quart canning jars, then pour in hot syrup to within ½ inch of the top. Seal with hot sterilized lids and rings. Process for 25 minutes in a boiling-water bath (see next page).

TO PROCESS in a boiling-water bath: Place a folded cloth in the bottom of a large pot or canning kettle and place each jar in the pot with tongs as you fill and seal it. Pour simmering water about halfway up the side of the jar. Add more jars, spacing them 1 inch apart to allow for heat circulation. When all the jars are in place, add boiling water to cover the lids by at least 1 inch. Bring the pot to a full, rolling boil over high heat, then start timing as directed in the recipe, maintaining a vigorous boil for the full time. When the time is up, lift the jars from the water with tongs and let cool on wire racks or newspaper on the counter. Avoid cool surfaces such as ceramic, tile, or marble; hot jars can break from thermal shock if brought into sudden contact with a cold surface.

AFTER THE JARS ARE COOL, check to see that the vacuum seal is complete. Place your forefinger on the lid and make sure it's depressed. If the lid will still "pop," it means you didn't get a good seal. Place this jar in the refrigerator and use the contents within a week or so. Wipe the jars, label them, and store in a cool, dark place.

SPICY PRESERVED PEAR CHUTNEY

*So good you could eat it with a spoon, spicy pear chutney sparks
Indian entrées, southern picnic suppers, and sandwiches. About one
quarter of the fruit by weight should be unripe for the best
pectin development.*

MAKES 5 PINTS

5 pounds Bartlett or Anjou pears,
cored, peeled, and coarsely
chopped (about 10 medium
pears)

2¼ cups (1 pound) packed light
brown sugar

2 cups (1 pound) granulated sugar

2⅔ cups (1 pound) golden raisins

3 garlic cloves, minced

2 tablespoons salt

2 tablespoons mustard seed

2 tablespoons red pepper flakes

1 tablespoon grated fresh ginger

1 tablespoon ground cumin

6 cups cider vinegar

COMBINE THE PEARS with the brown and white sugar in a large, heavy nonaluminum pan over medium-low heat. Bring the mixture slowly to a boil, then cook until thick, stirring from time to time, about 2 hours.

STIR IN ALL the remaining ingredients. Cover and bring the mixture to a boil over medium heat, then remove the pan from the heat, uncover, and let cool to room temperature. Cover and let stand overnight.

THE NEXT MORNING, bring the chutney mixture to a boil over medium-low heat and boil it slowly, uncovered, until reduced to about 5 pints, about 1 hour, stirring often. Spoon the mixture into hot sterilized jars and seal with hot sterilized lids.

PROCESS THE JARS in a boiling-water bath for 10 minutes (see page 73). Let cool, then label and date the jars. Store for at least 1 month in a cool, dark place before serving. This chutney will keep for up to 1 year in a cool, dark storage space.

5.

Breads and Desserts

German Pear Pancake

Pear-Rosemary Bread

Winter Pear and Orange Bread

Pear Focaccia

Five-Minute Pear Desserts

Basic Poached Pears

Crème de Cassis Sauce for Poached Pears

Cinnamon Poached Pears with Hot Fudge Sauce

Pears Belle Hélène

Poached Pears and Prunes in Red Wine

Jigsaw Pears with Custard Sauce

Ruby Red Stuffed Pears

Zinfandel Pears with California Bay Leaves

Braised Boscs in Butterscotch

Sugared Pears in Pecan Phyllo Purses

Brandied Pear Dumplings

Chunky French Pear Sauce

Pear Jumble Pie

Pear-Hazelnut Tart

Pear and Apricot Tart

Bosc Tarte Tatin

Impromptu Pear Pie

Comice Pear Pandowdy

German Pear Pudding

Pear-Cranberry Crisp

Seckel Upside-Down Cake

Lana Boldt's Pear Kuchen

Bartlett Ice Cream

Pear-Ginger Sorbet

GERMAN PEAR PANCAKE

Here's a pancake to comfort all ages. Try it with
link sausages. Be sure to pour the batter into a hot skillet so
the pancake will puff up beautifully. Don't forget to have lots of cold
milk to drink for the kids and hot tea for the grownups.

MAKES 4 SERVINGS

3 large eggs

½ teaspoon salt

½ cup unbleached all-purpose flour

½ cup milk

1 large ripe Bosc, Winter Nelis, or
   Anjou pear

2 tablespoons butter, plus ¼ cup
   melted butter for serving
   (optional)

Ground cinnamon and nutmeg for
   sprinkling

Maple syrup for serving

PREHEAT THE OVEN to 450°F. Place a 10-inch cast-iron skillet in the oven to heat.

USING A FOOD PROCESSOR fitted with the steel blade or a blender, whip the eggs for 1 minute, add the salt, flour, and milk, and process 1 minute longer. To make by hand, whip the eggs in a medium bowl using a wire whisk for about 1 minute, then add the salt, flour, and milk and beat for 2 more minutes.

USE A MELON BALLER to remove the core of the pear, leaving the peel on and the stem attached. Cut the pear into thin slices.

REMOVE THE HOT SKILLET from the oven and melt the 2 tablespoons butter in it. Fan pear slices over the bottom and quickly pour the batter onto the pears. Sprinkle with cinnamon and nutmeg, then pop the skillet into the hot oven. Bake the pancake until puffed and brown, about 15 minutes.

TO SERVE, cut the pancake into wedges and serve with the optional melted butter and the maple syrup.

PEAR-ROSEMARY BREAD

*A sweet-savory loaf that simply begs
for a smear of mascarpone cheese for dessert.*

MAKES ONE 8½-BY-4½-INCH LOAF

2 cups unbleached all-purpose flour
2 teaspoons baking powder
¼ teaspoon baking soda
¼ teaspoon salt
1 pound Bartlett, Comice, or Anjou
    pears (about 2 medium pears)
    cored, peeled, and chopped
2 teaspoons chopped fresh rosemary
Grated zest of ½ lemon
1 tablespoon fresh lemon juice
6 tablespoons (¾ stick) unsalted
    butter at room temperature
⅓ cup plus 1 tablespoon sugar
2 large eggs
1 fresh rosemary sprig

PREHEAT THE OVEN to 350°F.
Coat an 8½-by-4½-inch loaf pan with
vegetable-oil cooking spray. Dust the
pan lightly with flour. Set aside.
COMBINE THE FLOUR, baking
powder, baking soda, and salt together
in a food processor bowl fitted with
the steel blade. Pulse 10 times to aerate the flour, then transfer the mixture
to a sheet of waxed paper. Or, mix in a
bowl with a wire whisk.

IN A FOOD PROCESSOR fitted with
the steel blade or in a blender, process
the pears to a smooth purée. Stir the
rosemary, lemon zest, and lemon juice
into the pears.

BEAT THE BUTTER and the ⅓ cup
sugar in a medium bowl until creamy.
Beat in the eggs, one at a time. (Don't
worry if the mixture looks curdled
now.) Alternately, stir in the pear
purée and the flour mixture, mixing
only until all the flour is blended in.

POUR THE BATTER into the prepared pan and bake for 20 minutes.
Dip the rosemary sprig in water, then
in the 1 tablespoon sugar, and place
the sprig on top of the loaf. Continue
baking another 35 to 40 minutes, or
until the loaf is brown and springs
back at the touch.

LET COOL IN THE PAN on a rack
for 15 minutes, then unmold and let
cool to room temperature on the rack.
Wrap the loaf in plastic and store
overnight before slicing.

WINTER PEAR AND ORANGE BREAD

*A sweet zesty bread to toast
for brunch or to serve with afternoon tea.*

MAKES ONE 9-BY-5-INCH LOAF

1 unpeeled, underripe, Anjou, Bosc,
  or Winter Nelis pear, quartered
  and cored
1 teaspoon fresh lemon juice
Grated zest of ½ orange
½ cup fresh orange juice
1 cup sugar
2 eggs
½ cup vegetable oil
3 cups unbleached all-purpose flour
1 tablespoon baking powder
½ teaspoon baking soda
1½ teaspoons salt
1 teaspoon ground cinnamon
½ teaspoon ground nutmeg

PREHEAT THE OVEN to 350°F.
Coat a 9-by-5-inch loaf pan with vegetable-oil cooking spray.
FIT A FOOD PROCESSOR with the
grating disk and grate the pear. Or,
grate it with a hand grater. Measure
out ½ cup grated pear and place it in a
medium bowl. Sprinkle the lemon

juice over the remaining grated pear
and set it aside.
POUR THE ORANGE ZEST and
juice over the ½ cup grated pear. Add
the sugar, eggs, and oil. Whip with a
fork to mix thoroughly. Set aside.
COMBINE all the remaining ingredients in a large bowl. Stir with a fork to
aerate and mix the dry ingredients.
Pour the pear-orange mixture over the
dry ingredients. Mix with the fork just
until the ingredients are blended. Turn
this stiff batter into the prepared loaf
pan. Bake the loaf on the middle rack
of the oven for about 1 hour, or until it
is golden brown on top (don't worry if
it cracks) and a toothpick or wooden
skewer inserted in the center comes
out clean. Serve slices of bread with a
dollop of the reserved grated pear for
a zesty garnish.
LET IT COOL in the pan on a rack for
5 minutes, then unmold and let cool
on the rack. Serve warm or at room
temperature.

PEAR FOCACCIA

This flat yeast bread topped with fanned pear slices
makes a great brunch or tea centerpiece. Learn this processor method for
making yeast dough and you'll never do it any other way.

MAKES 4 TO 6 SERVINGS

3 cups bread flour

2 teaspoons salt

1 package (2½ teaspoons) active
    rapid-rise yeast

⅞ cup hot (120°F) water

2 tablespoons olive oil, plus more for
    coating

2 large ripe pears

Julienned zest of ½ lemon

1 teaspoon fresh lemon juice

1 teaspoon ground cinnamon

1 teaspoon turbinado sugar

1 tablespoon olive oil

PREHEAT THE OVEN to 500°F. (If using a baking stone or unglazed cooking tiles, place them on a shelf in the bottom third of the oven and preheat for 30 minutes.)

COMBINE THE FLOUR, salt, and yeast in a food processor fitted with the steel blade. Pulse to mix. Then, with the motor running, pour the hot water and olive oil through the feed tube. Process until the dough begins to leave the sides of the bowl. Knead for 60 seconds, adding flour as necessary if the dough seems sticky. Remove the blade and the dough from the processor. Knead the dough on a lightly floured surface a moment, then roll it into a ball and punch a hole in the middle, like a doughnut. Replace the dough in the processor bowl. Cover the bowl with plastic wrap. Place in a warm, draft-free place and let rise until doubled in bulk, about 45 minutes. Or, to micro-rise, set a microwave oven setting to 10 percent power, place an 8-ounce glass of water in the back, and add the dough in the processor bowl. Heat for 3 minutes,

(continued)

let rest for 3 minutes, heat for 3 minutes, and let rest for 6 minutes. The dough will now be doubled in bulk. REMOVE THE DOUGH from the processor bowl, punch it down, knead by hand a few seconds on a lightly floured board, then cover with the processor bowl and let it rest for 10 minutes.

ROLL THE FOCACCIA into an irregular 12- to 14-inch round. Transfer it to a cornmeal-sprinkled 15-inch baking sheet or a baker's peel (if using a pizza stone or tiles). Let the dough rise in a warm draft-free place until puffy, about 15 minutes.

MEANWHILE, core, peel, and cut the pears into thin slices and toss with the lemon zest and juice. Stir in the cinnamon and turbinado sugar.

DIMPLE THE TOP of the focaccia with your fingertips and brush with the olive oil. Arrange the pears and juice atop the raised focaccia. Place the baking sheet on the middle rack of the oven or shovel the focaccia from the baker's peel onto the preheated stone or tiles. Reduce heat to 400°F and bake for 15 minutes, or until golden brown. Cool it on a rack. Cut into wedges and serve warm or at room temperature.

FIVE-MINUTE PEAR DESSERTS

*Nothing is quite so elegant as a perfect pear,
unadorned, sitting in the middle of a fine dessert plate and presented
with only the proper cutlery. But sometimes
we like to gild the lily — just a bit.*

MAKES 2 SERVINGS

❋ The best bottle of Sauternes you can find, a wedge of Roquefort, and a perfect pear for each person.

❋ Halve, core, and peel 2 ripe Bartlett pears and place them on 2 dessert plates. Add a scoop or two of vanilla ice cream, drizzle with your favorite chocolate sauce, and top with a dollop of crème fraîche or sour cream. The combination of rich, sweet, sour, cold, and dark tastes beats the heck out of a banana split.

❋ Halve, core, and peel 2 ripe Anjou pears and place them on a pie plate. Sprinkle with rum, brown sugar, and lemon juice, then run them under a preheated broiler until they're bubbly and hot, about 3 minutes. Top with a dollop of whipped cream and serve on dessert plates.

❋ Core and peel 2 ripe whole Comice pears, then cut off the bottom so they'll sit up straight. Drizzle them with eau-de-vie (pear brandy), top with vanilla ice cream, and drizzle hot fudge sauce over it.

❋ Gouge out pear balls from a ripe Comice, Seckel, and Bosc pear. Toss the balls with fresh mint leaves and Champagne, then sprinkle with sugar and Cognac and serve.

❋ Peel, core, and section 2 ripe Comice pears, then dip them in chocolate sauce and serve. Or, dip them in Cognac. Add a dollop of vanilla ice cream.

❋ Core, peel, and cut up 1 Bartlett pear, 1 banana, 1 apple, and 1 orange, then toss them with toasted coconut and fresh orange juice.

❋ Toss 2 cored and peeled ripe Bartlett or Comice pears in balsamic vinegar and pepper lightly.

(continued)

TOASTING FLAKED or shredded coconut: To toast coconut in a microwave, sprinkle the coconut evenly into a 9-inch glass pie plate. Microwave on Medium (70 percent power) for 4 to 5 minutes for 1 cup coconut, or until the coconut begins to turn a light brown. It continues to cook once you've removed it from the microwave, so don't overdo it. Toss it with a fork once or twice while it's toasting and once or twice again after removing it from the microwave. Store in an airtight container for up to 1 month. Or, in a preheated 350°F oven or a toaster oven, toast coconut for 3 to 5 minutes, or until it begins to turn a light brown.

* Cut 2 wedges of fine blue cheese, place each on a bed of blueberries, add ½ ripe Bartlett or Comice pear to each serving, then drizzle all with port. Offer thin-sliced French bread.

* Cut 2 wedges of soft-ripe Brie, place each on a bed of raspberries, and add ½ ripe Bartlett pear to each serving. Offer thin-sliced French bread.

* Pour a little rum on 2 dessert plates. Core, peel, and slice 2 ripe Anjou or Comice pears and use each as a base for a snowball of vanilla ice cream rolled in toasted coconut (see below).

* Thinly slice pecorino cheese onto 2 dessert plates and top each with 1 cored, peeled, and quartered ripe Comice pear. Warm a little honey and drizzle it over. Sprinkle with freshly ground pepper.

BASIC POACHED PEARS

A pear cooked gently in perfumed water is dessert as old as Rome.
Use white wine or apple juice instead of plain water if you wish. You may
also poach pears in a microwave. A sprig of mint
at the stem end makes a fitting garnish.

MAKES 6 POACHED PEARS

6 firm, ripe Bartlett, Bosc, or Anjou
    pears
Juice of ½ lemon in a large bowl of
    water
½ cup water
½ cup dry white wine or apple,
    cranberry, or white grape juice
¼ cup fresh lemon juice
Julienned zest of ½ lemon
1 cup sugar

LEAVING THE STEM INTACT, core and peel the whole pears carefully, using a melon baller to remove the pear core from the bottom (see page 16). Cut a thin strip off the bottom off the pears so they will stand up firmly. Drop the pears into the lemon water so the pears won't darken.

COMBINE all the remaining ingredients in a medium-large nonaluminum or microwavable saucepan. Raise the mixture to a boil, then add the pears so they stand upright. Lower the liquid to a simmer, cover, and poach gently until the pears are just barely tender, no more than 10 to 15 minutes on top of the stove, or cook in a microwave on High (100 percent power) for about 10 minutes or until tender. Remove from heat, spoon the syrup over the pears again, and set aside to cool.

ONCE THE PEARS ARE COOL, cover, and refrigerate until needed. They'll keep for 3 to 4 days. Serve with chocolate or raspberry sauce, a dollop of whipped cream, or a little of your favorite berry or apricot jam.

CRÈME DE CASSIS SAUCE FOR POACHED PEARS

Pears poached in a lemony syrup are chilled and served in a pool of this garnet-colored sauce.

MAKES 4 SERVINGS, OR ABOUT 1 CUP

One 10-ounce package frozen
    blackberries, thawed
¼ cup black currant jam
3 tablespoons poaching liquid from
    Basic Poached Pears (recipe on
    page 85)
2½ teaspoons cornstarch
2 tablespoons crème de Cassis liqueur

PURÉE THE BERRIES in a food processor, blender, or food mill, then strain into a medium bowl. Mix the jam, poaching liquid, and purée in a medium saucepan. Mix the cornstarch with the liqueur in a cup and add it to the berry mixture. Mix well and simmer gently until the sauce is thick enough to coat the back of a spoon, about 10 minutes. Cover and chill.

SERVE EACH PEAR on a dessert dish in a pool of sauce. Garnish with a sprig of mint or rosemary leaves.

CINNAMON POACHED PEARS WITH HOT FUDGE SAUCE

The microwave is made for poaching pears and for making chocolate syrups. It provides easy clean-up and foolproof cooking. You may alter the poaching liquid in this recipe by substituting fruit juices — cranberry, apple, orange — or by adding spirits — triple sec, framboise, eau-de-vie.

MAKES 4 SERVINGS

2 cups water

¾ cup sugar

2 tablespoons fresh lemon juice

Julienned zest of ½ lemon

One 3-inch piece cinnamon stick

2 whole cloves

4 firm, ripe Bosc, Anjou, or Bartlett pears

Hot Fudge Sauce (see page 120)

4 fresh mint leaves for garnish

Microwave Method

IN A 2-QUART microwavable casserole, mix the water, sugar, lemon juice, zest, cinnamon, and whole cloves. Cover and microwave on High (100 percent power) for 4 minutes.

MEANWHILE, leaving the stems on, core the pears through the bottom using a small melon baller, then peel them. Cut a thin slice off the bottom so the pears will stand up. Place the pears in the hot syrup, spooning syrup over the pears to coat thoroughly. Cover and microwave on High (100 percent power) for about 10 minutes, turning the dish after 5 minutes. Spoon the syrup over the pears again, cover and let them cool in the syrup. Refrigerate overnight.

Conventional Method

MIX THE WATER, sugar, lemon juice and zest, cinnamon stick, and cloves in a medium nonaluminum pan and boil 4 to 5 minutes, then add the cored and trimmed pears (see above). Cover and poach for 10 to 12 minutes, or until pears are tender.

TO SERVE, puddle a little sauce onto dessert plates. Top each with a poached pear, then spoon 1 tablespoon of sauce over the top. Garnish with a mint leaf.

PEARS BELLE HÉLÈNE

A classic French way with pears:
luscious poached pears drenched in chocolate sauce and served
with ice cream. Frozen yogurt makes for a lighter dish.

MAKES 4 SERVINGS

4 ripe Anjou or Bartlett pears
½ cup water
2 tablespoons sugar
1 teaspoon vanilla extract
1 cup vanilla ice cream or frozen
    nonfat yogurt
Bittersweet Cocoa Sauce (see page
    120)
Fresh mint leaves for garnish

CORE THE PEARS from the bottom using a small melon baller, then peel, leaving the stem intact. Cut a slice off the bottom of each pear. Combine the water, sugar, and vanilla in a large saucepan and bring to a boil. Set the pears in the syrup, cover, and reduce heat to a simmer, then poach the pears until tender, about 10 minutes. Remove from the heat and let the pears cool in the syrup for 1 hour. Serve now or cover and refrigerate several hours or overnight.

TO SERVE, place each pear in a dessert dish in a pool of Bittersweet Cocoa Sauce. Nestle a scoop of ice cream or frozen yogurt next to the pear, drizzle additional sauce over the pear and ice cream or frozen yogurt, and garnish with a mint leaf.

POACHED PEARS AND PRUNES
IN RED WINE

*Peppercorns give this dessert a little zip, the lemon juice
adds a little tang, and the honey provides a sweet smoothness that
will make you wish for more. Poach the pears and prunes in this perfumed
nectar, then marinate overnight for the maximum zing.*

MAKES 4 SERVINGS

Poaching Liquid

3 cups dry red wine

2 cups water

¾ cup packed dark brown sugar

1 cinnamon stick

10 peppercorns

¼ cup honey

1 teaspoon vanilla extract

Juice of ½ lemon

4 firm, ripe Bartlett or Bosc pears

12 jumbo prunes, pitted

Fresh mint sprigs for garnish

COMBINE THE WINE, water, brown sugar, cinnamon, peppercorns, honey, vanilla, and lemon juice in a large microwavable dish. Add the squeezed lemon half to the wine. Microwave on High (100 percent power) for 5 minutes. Or, cook on the stovetop in a medium saucepan for 10 minutes.

LEAVING THE STEMS INTACT, core the pears from the bottom with a small melon baller. Peel the pears and cut a thin slice off the bottom of each pear so that the pear will stand upright in the liquid. Add the pears and prunes to the poaching liquid. Lower a microwavable plate into the container to weight the pears under the liquid. Poach the pears on High (100 percent power) until tender, about 10 minutes. Or, poach the pears in the liquid in the saucepan until tender, about 10 minutes. Remove the plate and let the pears and prunes cool in the poaching liquid.

LIFT THE PEARS, prunes, and lemon half from the poaching liquid. Discard the lemon. Boil the poaching liquid in the microwave set at High (100 percent power) to reduce it by half, about 3 minutes.

OR, REDUCE in a saucepan on the stovetop for 5 minutes or so until the syrup is thick. Pour the thick syrup over the pears and prunes. Cover and refrigerate overnight. To serve, place 1 pear and 3 prunes on each plate. Garnish with a sprig of mint and serve.

JIGSAW PEARS WITH CUSTARD SAUCE

*Jim Fobel, one of America's premier recipe developers
and cooks, developed this recipe for a New York food show. He taught me
the zigzag presentation. Other filling possibilities:
cherries, raspberries, a few raisins.*

MAKES 6 SERVINGS

½ cup water
½ cup apple juice or bourbon
¼ cup fresh lemon juice
½ cup firmly packed brown sugar
6 firm, large ripe pears
12 walnut halves
Custard Sauce (see page 122)
Fresh mint sprigs for garnish

COMBINE THE WATER, apple juice or bourbon, lemon juice, and brown sugar in a microwavable casserole that is deep enough for the pears to stand upright; microwave on High (100 percent power) for 3 minutes. Stir to completely dissolve the sugar; set aside.

MEANWHILE, leaving the stems intact, carefully peel the pears, cut the bottom off flat so the pears will stand upright. Stand the uncored pears in the casserole and spoon the hot syrup over them. Cover and microwave on High (100 percent power) for 10 minutes.

OR, COMBINE the poaching ingredients in a large saucepan and bring to a boil. Set the pears in the syrup, cover, and reduce heat to a simmer, then poach the pears until tender, about 10 minutes. Remove the cover and spoon the syrup over the pears again.

ALLOW THE PEARS to cool to room temperature, then cover and refrigerate until serving time.

CAREFULLY CUT the chilled pears in half crosswise in a zigzag pattern. Remove the core with a small melon baller and stuff each hollow with 2 walnut halves. Fit the pears back together. Stand each pear on a dessert plate in a pool of custard sauce. Add a sprig of mint to the top of each pear.

RUBY RED
STUFFED PEARS

*If you can find red-skinned Bartletts, Comices, or Anjous,
use them; the color of the finished dessert will be an even deeper crimson.
This dessert is a fitting end to a holiday meal.*

MAKES 8 SERVINGS

1 quart water

2 cups granulated sugar

1 vanilla bean, split lengthwise

8 ripe Red Comice, Bartlett, or Anjou
    pears

One 8-ounce package cream cheese at
    room temperature

¼ cup powdered sugar

½ teaspoon almond extract

3 tablespoons almonds, toasted (see
    page 28) and finely chopped

One 10-ounce package frozen
    raspberries in syrup

2 tablespoons Chambord

1 lemon, halved

8 fresh mint leaves

LEAVING THE STEMS and skin on the pears, cut off the bottom so they'll stand upright in the pan. Core the pears from the bottom using a melon baller to remove the seeds and to leave a large opening for the stuffing.

COMBINE THE WATER, sugar and vanilla bean in a large stockpot and bring to a boil. Stir the boiling syrup to dissolve the sugar, then reduce the heat and add the pears. Cover and cook gently until the pears are tender, about 10 minutes. Let the pears cool in the syrup, then cover and refrigerate for 24 hours.

COMBINE THE CREAM CHEESE, powdered sugar, and almond extract in a food processor fitted with a steel blade, a blender, or a small bowl and blend until smooth. Add the chopped almonds and pulse 2 or 3 times or blend with a spoon.

PRESS THE RASPBERRIES and syrup through a fine-meshed sieve and discard the pulp and seeds. Stir the Chambord into the raspberry syrup and refrigerate until serving time.

TO SERVE, remove the pears from the syrup. Gently stuff the pears from the bottom with the cream cheese mixture. You may pipe it in using a pastry bag or a self-sealing plastic bag with a hole snipped in one corner, or you may simply push it in with your finger. Pool some raspberry syrup on each dessert plate and place a pear upright in the raspberry syrup. Drizzle some additional syrup on top of each pear and garnish with a sprig of mint. Pour the remaining syrup into a pitcher and pass when serving.

ZINFANDEL PEARS
WITH CALIFORNIA BAY LEAVES

*Braising pears in butter before steeping them in a
clear red wine syrup with peppery bay leaves makes a fine Italian-style
dessert or a good side dish for roast meats.*

MAKES 4 SERVINGS

4 large ripe Bosc, Anjou, or Comice
    pears
2 tablespoons unsalted butter
6 tablespoons sugar
6 bay leaves
2 cups Zinfandel or other dry red wine

LEAVING THE STEMS INTACT, core the pears from the bottom with a melon baller. Peel the pears, then cut them in half lengthwise. Heat the butter in a 12-inch skillet until it foams, then sauté the pears, flat-side down, until golden. Turn the pears and sauté the rounded side for 5 minutes, or until golden. Add the sugar, then spread the bay leaves in the pan and pour in the wine. Cover and reduce heat to medium. Cook the pears until tender, about 10 to 15 minutes. Using a slotted spoon, lift the pears from the liquid to a serving dish. Discard the bay leaves.

RAISE THE HEAT to high and boil the syrup to reduce it until it is thick and deep red in color, about 5 to 8 minutes. Pour 1 tablespoon of the hot syrup over each pear and serve at once. Pour the remaining syrup in a pitcher and pass it. If you have syrup left over, it makes a divine topping for vanilla ice cream.

BRAISED BOSCS IN BUTTERSCOTCH

The long, graceful Bosc pear, halved and
braised in butterscotch sauce, makes a splendid dessert.
Served with the warm sauce and topped with vanilla ice cream,
it's the perfect end to a winter meal.

MAKES 8 SERVINGS

4 ripe Bosc pears

Juice of ½ lemon in a large bowl of
water

¾ cup packed brown sugar

2 tablespoons unsalted butter

¼ cup water

Vanilla ice cream

PREHEAT THE OVEN TO 350°F.
Halve and core the pears, then peel.
Drop the pears into the bowl of lemon
water to prevent darkening.

COMBINE THE BROWN SUGAR,
butter, and water in an 11-by-7-inch
glass baking dish. Microwave on High
(100 percent power) for 3 minutes,
stirring once after 1½ minutes to dissolve the brown sugar. Alternatively,
boil the ingredients for 3 minutes in a
saucepan, then transfer to the baking
dish.

ARRANGE THE PEAR HALVES,
cut-side up, in the baking dish and
spoon the butterscotch over them.
Cover the dish with aluminum foil and
braise in the preheated oven for 30
minutes. Remove the foil, turn the
pears over, spoon the butterscotch
over them again, and bake for 10 more
minutes.

TO SERVE, place 1 pear half on each
dessert plate, cut-side up. Scoop some
butterscotch sauce over the pear, then
add a spoonful of vanilla ice cream.

SUGARED PEARS IN PECAN PHYLLO PURSES

This golden dessert is a feast for the eyes. Each crispy purse is served in its baking bowl on a dessert plate and garnished with a sprig of mint. This dessert can be made hours ahead; simply reheat the sauce at the last moment and spoon it over the pears.

MAKES 6 SERVINGS

Filling

Julienned zest of 1 lemon

¼ cup fresh lemon juice

2 cups water

6 large ripe Bartlett or Comice pears

⅔ cup sugar

⅓ cup unbleached all-purpose flour

½ teaspoon ground cinnamon

⅓ cup cold butter

1 large egg, lightly beaten

¾ cup fresh orange juice

Pecan Phyllo Purses

1½ cups (6 ounces) pecan halves or pieces

⅓ cup sugar

1¼ teaspoons julienned lemon zest

1 teaspoon ground cinnamon

12 sheets (8 ounces) fresh or thawed frozen phyllo pastry

12 fresh mint leaves for garnish

½ cup fresh orange juice

PREHEAT THE OVEN to 350°F. Coat a 9-by-13-inch flameproof baking dish with vegetable-oil spray. Coat six 4½-inch ovenproof baking dishes or individual soufflé dishes with vegetable-oil spray and set aside.

TO MAKE THE FILLING: Combine the lemon zest, juice, and water in a medium bowl. Core and peel the pears, leaving stems intact, and add them, turning to coat all sides. Set aside.

COMBINE THE SUGAR, flour, and cinnamon in a food processor fitted with the plastic blade. Place the butter on top of the flour. Pulse to mix until butter is about the size of lima beans (5 to 6 pulses). Or, to mix by hand, combine the sugar, flour and cinnamon in a medium bowl and stir to mix. Cut the butter into small pieces and add to the flour mixture. Mix with an electric mixer or your hands until the mixture resembles peas or lima beans. Pour the mixture onto a piece of waxed paper.

DRAIN THE PEARS and pat them dry with paper towels. Roll the pears in the beaten egg, then dredge them in the sugar-flour mixture. Place in the prepared baking dish, stem-side up, then pour the orange juice under the pears and bake, uncovered, for 1 hour, or until tender. Remove the pears, reserving the juices in the dish.

WHILE THE PEARS are cooking, make the phyllo purses. Process the pecans with the sugar, lemon zest, and cinnamon in a food processor fitted with the steel blade until the nuts are the size of peas. Or, chop by hand.

STACK THE PHYLLO SHEETS on a damp towel. Using kitchen shears or a sharp French chef's knife, cut the phyllo in half lengthwise, then cut each portion in half crosswise, forming 48 rectangles. Place 6 rectangles on the countertop and coat them with vegetable-oil cooking spray, then place 1 rectangle in each small baking dish. Stack the remaining rectangles on a damp towel and cover with a damp towel. Repeat the procedure 3 more times, placing each succeeding rectangle at an angle to the last one. Press the phyllo down into each dish with your fingertips so that the purse is formed.

SPOON ABOUT 1½ tablespoons of the pecan mixture into each shell. Top each with 2 phyllo rectangles coated with vegetable-oil cooking spray and placed at alternating angles. Repeat, using the remaining pecan mixture and phyllo rectangles, again, pressing the phyllo into the dishes. Bake for 10 to 12 minutes, or until the top edges are golden. Let cool in the baking dishes on racks.

GENTLY PLACE 1 cooked pear in each purse. Add the ½ cup orange juice to the pan juices and cook, stirring, over medium-high heat until the sauce is thick, about 5 minutes. You may complete the recipe up to this point 6 hours before serving.

TO SERVE, warm the sauce, drizzle a little over each pear, and top with mint leaves. Pour the remaining sauce into a pitcher and pass it around.

BRANDIED PEAR
DUMPLINGS

*A glamour dessert, stuffed pears are wrapped in
pastry ribbons and topped with sugared pastry leaves.
Easy, good, and gorgeous.*

MAKES 4 SERVINGS

Filling

2 tablespoons finely chopped dried
    apricots
1 tablespoon finely chopped hazelnuts
2 tablespoons low-fat whipped cream
    cheese

4 medium ripe Anjou, Bartlett, or
    Bosc pears
1 recipe pie crust (see page 105)
4 whole cloves
1 large egg white
1 tablespoon water
1 tablespoon sugar
1 cup pear nectar
¼ cup dark corn syrup
¼ cup pear eau-de-vie (pear brandy)
    or additional pear nectar
Half-and-half for serving

PREHEAT THE OVEN to 400°F.
Coat a glass pie plate with vegetable-
oil cooking spray and set it aside. Make
the filling in a small bowl by combin-
ing the apricots, hazelnuts, and cream
cheese. Mash together with a fork.

LEAVING THE STEMS INTACT,
core the pears from the bottom using a
melon baller and leaving a large opening in the bottom for the filling. Peel
the pears, then stuff each one from the
bottom with the apricot-nut mixture.

ROLL THE PASTRY DOUGH out
into a 13-inch circle on a lightly
floured board. Trim to a 12-inch
square. Using a fluted pastry wheel or
a knife, cut the dough into fourteen
12-by-¾-inch strips.

DRY THE PEARS with paper towels.
Using 3 strips for each pear, wrap the
fruit in pastry, starting about ½ inch
above the base of the pear. Moisten the
end of the first strip and seal the end of
the second pastry strip onto it. Continue with a third pastry strip to cover
the top, allowing the pear's stem to
protrude through the top.

(continued)

USE A SHARP PARING knife to cut diamond-shaped leaves from the remaining 2 pastry strips. Mark veins on the leaves using the point of the knife. Attach 2 leaves to the top of each pear on either side of the stem, moistening the pastry with water so it will stick properly. If necessary, use broken toothpicks to hold the leaves in place. Finish with a clove stuck in beside the stem of the pear. Stir together the egg white and water and brush it all over the pastry. Sprinkle generously with sugar.

USE A SPATULA to transfer the pears to a glass pie plate. Stir together the nectar, syrup, and brandy. Pour this mixture into the bottom of the pie plate. Bake, uncovered, for 45 to 50 minutes, or until the pears are golden brown. Serve warm in a pool of half-and-half.

CHUNKY FRENCH PEAR SAUCE

Use slightly underripe pears for a sauce that holds its shape. Summer or winter pears may be used for this sauce with equal success.

MAKES 3 CUPS

8 underripe Bartlett, Anjou, or Bosc pears

Juice of ½ lemon in a large bowl of water

3 tablespoons unsalted butter

Julienned zest and juice of ½ lemon

¼ cup sugar

2 tablespoons pear eau-de-vie (pear brandy), optional

CORE, PEEL, QUARTER, and cut the pears into wedges. As you prepare the fruit, drop the pear wedges into the bowl of lemon juice to keep the fruit from darkening. Heat the butter in a large nonstick skillet over medium-high heat, then add the pear wedges, turning them to coat all sides with butter. Add the lemon zest and juice. Cover and reduce heat to a simmer. Cook just until the pears are tender, about 10 to 20 minutes.

STIR IN THE SUGAR and continue to cook until the mixture thickens and nearly all the liquid has evaporated, about 10 minutes. Turn off heat and stir in the eau-de-vie. Serve warm or cold.

PEAR JUMBLE PIE

If a little streusel's good, then a lot's bound to be
mouthwatering. In this single-crust pie, streusel is both a bed and
topping for the chopped and fanned pears. Use Bartletts in the summer and
Anjous or Boscs in the winter for a luscious, homey dessert.

MAKES ONE 9-INCH DEEP-DISH PIE; SERVES 8

1 unbaked 9-inch deep dish pie crust
    (see page 105)
⅔ cup packed dark brown sugar
¼ cup unbleached all-purpose flour
¼ cup uncooked rolled oats
1 teaspoon ground ginger
1 teaspoon ground cinnamon
¼ cup (½ stick) butter, cut into small
    pieces
6 medium ripe Bartlett or Bosc pears
Julienned zest and juice of 1 lemon

PREHEAT THE OVEN to 375°F.
Fit the pie crust into a 9-inch pie pan,
trim and flute the edges, and set it
aside.

COMBINE THE BROWN SUGAR,
flour, rolled oats, ginger, and cinnamon in a medium bowl. Cut in the
butter until the mixture resembles
coarse crumbs. Sprinkle about half the
mixture (about ¾ cup) into the pie
pan. Core, peel, and halve the pears.
Coarsely chop 4 of the pear halves and
toss them with the lemon zest and half
the lemon juice. Scatter this mixture
over the crumbs.

CUT EACH OF 7 PEAR halves into
¼-inch-thick lengthwise slices from
the wide end almost to the stem end.
Arrange each half on the crumb-pear
mixture with the wide ends of the
pears toward the edge of the pie. Gently press down on the pear halves to
fan the slices. Chop up the remaining
pear half and place it in the center.
Sprinkle the remaining lemon juice
over the pears, then sprinkle with the
remaining half of the crumbs.

BAKE ON THE BOTTOM shelf of
the oven for 40 to 45 minutes, or until
the crumbs are browned and the pears
are tender. Let cool on a rack. Serve at
room temperature.

PEAR-HAZELNUT TART

A gorgeous dessert of puff pastry filled with aromatic pears and hazelnuts makes it seem as if you just got back from a week at a French cooking school. The effort is worth it. This dessert's a knockout.

MAKES 8 SERVINGS

One 16-ounce package frozen puff
    pastry

Hazelnut Cream
½ cup hazelnuts, toasted and peeled
    (see page 28)
9 tablespoons sugar
1 cup milk
⅛ teaspoon salt
2 large egg yolks
2 tablespoons cornstarch
2 tablespoons unsalted butter
1½ teaspoons vanilla extract

2 ripe Bosc, Anjou or Bartlett pears,
    cored, peeled, and quartered
1 large egg
1 tablespoon water

THAW THE PUFF PASTRY at room temperature. Line 2 baking sheets with parchment paper. Divide the thawed puff pastry in half. Roll one half into a 10½-inch piece on a lightly floured board. Using a 10-inch plate as a guide, trim the pastry to a 10-inch circle. Transfer this pastry to a parchment-lined baking sheet and refrigerate. Roll the remaining pastry to a 12½-inch piece. Using a 12-inch plate, trim it to a 12-inch piece. Transfer this to the other parchment paper–lined baking sheet. Mark the center of the circle and punch a ½-inch circle in the dough using a doughnut cutter or a sharp knife. Refrigerate this sheet of pastry as well.

MEANWHILE, make the hazelnut cream: Place the hazelnuts in a blender or a food processor fitted with the steel blade. Process with 1 tablespoon of the sugar until the nuts are finely ground. Set aside. In a medium saucepan, combine the milk, 6 tablespoons of the sugar, and the salt. Bring the mixture to a boil.

(continued)

WHISK THE EGG YOLKS, remaining 2 tablespoons sugar, and the cornstarch in a medium bowl. Gradually whisk the hot milk mixture into the eggs, then return this mixture to the saucepan and continue cooking until the mixture becomes thick, about 1 minute. Remove from heat and stir in the butter and vanilla. Transfer the mixture to the medium bowl and cover with plastic wrap pressed onto the surface of the pudding. Chill in an ice-water bath or the refrigerator for about 30 minutes. Stir in the ground nuts.

REMOVE THE 10-INCH pastry circle from the refrigerator and spread the cold hazelnut cream on top, leaving a 1-inch border. Cut each pear quarter lengthwise into 4 slices and fan the pears on top of the filling in a circle, with the stem ends of the pears meeting in the center. Arrange the remaining slices on top in another circle. Brush the pastry border with water.

Gently arrange the remaining pastry over the pears. Press the edges together to seal. With the blunt side of a paring knife, press the pastry edges at 1-inch intervals toward the center to form a scalloped edge. Freeze for 30 minutes.

PREHEAT THE OVEN to 425°F. Whisk the egg and water together in a cup. Brush over the tart. With a sharp paring knife, score the top about ⅛ inch deep in a spoke pattern beginning at the center and curving down to the scalloped edge. Bake for 10 minutes, then reduce heat to 350°F and continue baking until the tart is a deep golden color, about 30 minutes. Let cool on a rack. Cut into wedges and serve warm or at room temperature.

PEAR AND APRICOT TART

*This small mountain of a tart makes a perfect end
to a dinner for four. Use parchment paper under the tart
while it cooks and you're guaranteed that it will be easy to transfer
to a footed serving dish for a dramatic presentation.*

MAKES 4 SERVINGS

Crust

1 cup unbleached all-purpose flour

1 tablespoon sugar

¼ teaspoon salt

½ cup (1 stick) chilled unsalted
   butter, cut into pieces

¼ cup ice water

Filling

2 ripe Bartlett or Bosc pears (about
   1 pound)

Grated zest and juice of ½ lemon

4 tablespoons apricot jam

2 tablespoons unsalted butter, cut into
   small pieces

1 tablespoon sugar

Vanilla ice cream or whipped cream
   for garnish (optional)

PLACE THE FLOUR, sugar, and salt in a food processor fitted with the plastic blade. Pulse to mix. Dot the top with butter pieces. Pulse to mix just until the butter is the size of lima beans (about 5 pulses). With the motor running, dribble in the ice water just until the dough forms a loose ball that rides around the blade, no more than 10 seconds. To make the crust by hand, see page 108.

SCOOP UP THE PASTRY DOUGH and make a firm ball with your hands. Flatten into a disk. Wrap in plastic and refrigerate for 30 minutes.

PREHEAT THE OVEN to 350°F. Place a piece of parchment paper on a baking sheet and coat it lightly with vegetable-oil cooking spray.

CORE, PEEL, AND HALVE each pear lengthwise. Place in a bowl and drizzle with the zest and lemon juice to prevent darkening.

ROLL OUT THE CHILLED dough into an 9-inch circle on a lightly floured surface. Transfer the dough onto the parchment paper-covered baking sheet.

(continued)

PLACE THE PEARS, cut-side down, on the pie crust circle, necks facing the middle, forming a kind of square. Using a melon baller, scoop out a hole in the top of each pear and add 1 tablespoon of jam. Place the leftover pear balls in the middle of the pie. Dot with butter. Pull up the pie crust and pinch the edges shut, making a 4-sided mountain. Spritz the pastry with plain water, then sprinkle with sugar. Bake until golden, about 25 minutes. Remove the tart to a rack, leaving the parchment in place. Let cool a few minutes before serving, then slide the tart off the paper and onto a footed serving plate and serve warm. A scoop of vanilla ice cream or whipped cream is a nice garnish.

BOSC TARTE TATIN

The French Tatin sisters surely had no idea how famous their
luscious caramelized fruit tart would become. Winter and autumn dinners
are perfectly punctuated by a luscious caramelized fruit tart.

MAKES ONE 10-INCH PIE; SERVES 8

PREHEAT THE OVEN to 375°F. Position the rack in the bottom third of the oven.

TO MAKE THE PASTRY in a food processor: Combine the flour and salt in a food processor fitted with the plastic blade. Add the butter. Pulse 5 to 6 times until the butter is incorporated and only pea-sized pieces remain. Measure out 1 tablespoon egg yolk and mix it with the water in a small bowl. With the motor running, pour the mixture through the feed tube and process just until the dough begins to mass around the blade, no more than 10 seconds. Remove the dough from the bowl and gently press it into an 8-inch disk. Cover with plastic wrap and chill in the refrigerator for 10 to 15 minutes.

TO MAKE THE PASTRY by hand: Combine the flour and salt in a medium bowl. Add the butter bits and rub flour into the butter with your fingers, lifting the flour and letting it fall into the bowl like flakes until the mixture resembles small peas. Mix 1 tablespoon egg yolk with the water and pour it into the flour mixture. Mix

Pastry

1 cup unbleached all-purpose flour, plus additional for rolling the dough

½ teaspoon salt

½ cup (1 stick), chilled unsalted butter, cut into bits

1 tablespoon egg yolk

1 tablespoon water

Filling

6 large ripe Bosc pears

2 tablespoons fresh lemon juice

Grated zest of ½ lemon

¾ cup sugar

¼ cup (½ stick) unsalted butter

and squeeze until the mixture is wet and sticks together. Turn it into an 8-inch disk. Cover with plastic wrap and refrigerate for 10 to 15 minutes.

TO MAKE THE FILLING: Core and peel the pears, then halve them lengthwise, leaving the stems intact. Place them in a bowl and toss them with the lemon zest and juice.

PLACE THE SUGAR in a 10-inch, ovenproof, cast-iron skillet or tarte Tatin pan over low heat. Cook and stir until the sugar melts and turns a pale golden color, about 10 minutes. Remove the pan from the heat and arrange the pears in the pan, cut-side up and sides touching, with the necks of the pears toward the center. Fill in the middle with any remaining pears. Cut the butter into bits and scatter it over the pears. Place the pan over medium heat. Cook until the sugar turns a deep caramel color and the juices have nearly evaporated, 15 to 20 minutes.

WITH A HEAVY ROLLING PIN coated with flour, roll the dough into a ¼-inch-thick circle on a lightly floured work surface. Carefully lift the pastry over the rolling pin and transfer it to the fruit in the skillet. Roll the dough over the top of the skillet. Trim the dough with a sharp knife to ½ inch larger than the skillet. Tuck the over-hanging dough in and around the fruit. Bake until the crust is golden brown, about 25 to 30 minutes. Let cool on a rack for about 10 minutes before serving.

TO SERVE, choose a 12-inch or bigger flat plate. Run a small, sharp knife around the edge of the tart to loosen it. Place the flat plate on top of the skillet, then carefully and quickly flip the tart over onto the plate. Let it stand a few minutes before serving. Cut into wedges and serve with crème fraîche or vanilla ice cream, if desired.

IMPROMPTU PEAR PIE

*Here's a homey pear pie using a light crust with only
212 calories and 5.2 grams of fat per serving. The crust is rolled into
a circle bigger than the pie pan, filled, and the overhang
is folded back over the fruit and twisted shut.*

MAKES ONE 9-INCH PIE; SERVES 10

Lower-Fat Pastry

1½ cups unbleached all-purpose flour

1 tablespoon granulated sugar

¼ teaspoon salt

¼ cup (½ stick) unsalted butter, cut
    into 4 pieces

¼ cup ice water

Filling and Topping

4 pounds ripe Bosc, Anjou, or Bartlett
    pears, cored, peeled, and
    chopped (about 4 cups)

⅓ cup packed dark brown sugar

¼ cup cornstarch

⅛ teaspoon ground cloves

1 tablespoon granulated sugar

PREHEAT THE OVEN to 350°F.
Spray a 9-inch pie pan with vegetable-oil cooking spray.

COMBINE THE FLOUR, sugar, and the salt in a food processor fitted with the steel blade. Pulse to mix, then add the butter and pulse 10 times, or until the mixture resembles coarse meal. With the motor running, add ice water through the feed tube, processing until it forms a loose ball (count to 20 and it will be ready). Or, make the pastry by hand (see page 108)

USE YOUR HANDS to gather the dough into a disk, wrap it in plastic, then freeze for 5 minutes. On a lightly floured surface, roll the dough into a 13-inch circle. Drape the circle of dough over the rolling pin and transfer to the prepared pie pan. Fill with the fruit.

STIR TOGETHER the brown sugar, cornstarch, and cloves in a small bowl. Sprinkle over the fruit. Fold the crust back over the top of the filling, pinching the crust shut and folding it into a fan. The hole in the middle will act as a steam vent. Spray the top of the pie with vegetable-oil spray, then sprinkle with the granulated sugar.

BAKE FOR 45 minutes, or until lightly browned. Let cool for 20 minutes on a wire rack before cutting into wedges to serve.

COMICE PEAR PANDOWDY

*The pandowdy is an old New England dish, created to use
windfall fruits. Originally served for breakfast, it's good for Sunday brunch.
The partially baked crust is broken into pieces and pushed into the
fruit before returning it to the oven to finish baking.*

MAKES 4 SERVINGS

4 cups unpeeled, underripe Comice
    pears, cored and cut into ½-inch-
    thick slices
Grated zest and juice of ½ lemon
1 cup pear nectar

Crust and Topping
½ teaspoon ground cinnamon
½ teaspoon freshly grated nutmeg
1 cup unbleached all-purpose flour
¼ teaspoon salt
½ cup (1 stick) cold butter, cut into
    bits
3 tablespoons ice water
2 teaspoons milk
1 tablespoon sugar

Vanilla low-fat yogurt for serving

PREHEAT THE OVEN to 350°F.
Coat an 8-inch square pan with vegetable-oil cooking spray. Toss the pear
slices with the lemon juice and zest.
Place the pears in the prepared pan,
pour the nectar over, and set aside.

COMBINE THE CINNAMON, nut-
meg, flour, and salt in a food processor
fitted with steel blade. Pulse to mix.
Open the lid and add the butter.
Process until the mixture resembles
coarse meal, about 10 seconds. With
the motor running, pour the ice water
and milk through the feed tube.
Process just until the mixture is
crumbly. Or, to mix by hand, combine
the cinnamon, nutmeg, flour, and salt
in a medium bowl and stir to mix. Add
the butter bits and beat with an electric mixer or by hand until the mixture resembles coarse meal. Add the
water and the milk and beat until the
mixture is crumbly. Sprinkle this mixture over the pears. Sprinkle with
sugar.

BAKE UNTIL BUBBLY and brown,
about 30 minutes. Using a spoon, push
the crust down into the fruit and bake
10 minutes longer. To serve, cut into
4-inch squares and serve with a dollop
of yogurt.

GERMAN PEAR PUDDING

*A cross between a cake and a pudding, this traditional
German dessert is light and luscious. Serve the warm pudding-cake
in a dessert dish with a garnish of whipped cream.*

MAKES 8 SERVINGS

½ cup cake flour

¼ cup cornstarch

½ teaspoon baking powder

1 cup dry red wine

¾ cup sugar

Grated zest of ½ lemon

½ teaspoon ground cinnamon

2 whole cloves

4 large ripe Bosc, or Anjou pears,
    cored, peeled, and quartered

1 egg, separated

2 egg whites

3 tablespoons water

1 teaspoon vanilla extract

Whipped cream for garnish

PREHEAT OVEN to 375°F. Coat a 9-inch square cake pan with vegetable-oil cooking spray and set aside. Aerate the flour, cornstarch, and baking powder in a bowl with a wire whisk. Transfer to a piece of waxed paper.

COMBINE THE WINE, ¼ cup of the sugar, the lemon zest, cinnamon, and cloves in a medium saucepan and bring to a boil. Slip the pears into the hot liquid, reduce heat, cover, and simmer until the pears are tender, about 10 to 15 minutes. Lift the pears out of the liquid with a slotted spoon, drain and transfer to the baking pan. Strain 1 cup of the cooking liquid into the pan.

WHIP THE EGG WHITES in a medium bowl using an electric mixer or wire whisk until whites hold a soft peak. Fold in egg yolk, vanilla, and the remaining ½ cup sugar. Sprinkle the flour over the mixture and fold it in. Spread the mixture evenly over the pears.

BAKE UNTIL the topping springs back lightly and the top is golden, 30 to 35 minutes. Serve warm or cold with a garnish of whipped cream if desired.

PEAR-CRANBERRY CRISP

*Good for breakfast and
great after dinner, this easy sweet-tart crisp may be made
with less-than-picture-perfect pears.*

MAKES 9 SERVINGS

PREHEAT THE OVEN to 400°F. Coat a 9-inch square baking dish with vegetable-oil cooking spray and set aside.

½ cup unbleached all-purpose flour

½ cup packed light brown sugar

½ cup rolled oats

1 cup dried cranberries

1 teaspoon ground cinnamon

½ teaspoon ground cloves

¼ teaspoon ground nutmeg

2 pounds ripe Bosc, Seckel, or Anjou pears, cored, peeled, and chopped (4 cups)

¼ cup cranberry juice

¼ cup (½ stick) cold butter, chopped into bits

Cream or vanilla nonfat yogurt for serving

COMBINE THE FLOUR, brown sugar, and oats in a medium bowl. In a small bowl, toss the cranberries with the cinnamon, cloves, and nutmeg. Stir each mixture well.

STIR THE CRANBERRY MIXTURE in with the pears, then arrange the fruit at the bottom of the baking pan and pour the juice over the fruit. Cut the butter into the flour mixture until it resembles coarse crumbs. Sprinkle the flour-sugar mixture over the fruit.

BAKE ON THE MIDDLE RACK of the oven for 35 to 45 minutes, or until bubbly and brown. Remove to a rack and let cool for 20 minutes. Serve warm in bowls, with cream or vanilla nonfat yogurt.

SECKEL UPSIDE-DOWN CAKE

Little Seckels fit nicely into a cast-iron skillet to form the base for this fall dessert. Substitute Bosc, Anjou, or Comice pears if you wish.

MAKES 10 SERVINGS

¾ cup (1½ sticks) butter at room temperature

¼ cup packed brown sugar

6 ripe Seckel pears, cored, peeled, and halved

Julienned zest and juice of 1 orange (about ½ cup juice)

¼ cup chopped crystallized ginger

½ cup pecan halves

1 cup granulated sugar

1 large egg

1½ teaspoons vanilla extract

2 teaspoons baking powder

½ teaspoon salt

1⅔ cups cake flour

½ cup milk

PREHEAT THE OVEN to 350°F. Melt ¼ cup of the butter in a 10-inch cast-iron skillet. Sprinkle the brown sugar over the butter. Arrange the pear halves, cut-side down, in the skillet. Sprinkle the orange zest, juice, crystallized ginger, and pecans over the pears and set aside.

IN A LARGE BOWL, cream the remaining ½ cup butter with the granulated sugar, egg, and vanilla. Stir the baking powder, salt, and flour together. Add the dry mixture to the butter mixture alternately with the milk, mixing until the batter is smooth.

POUR THE MIXTURE evenly over the pears. Bake for 45 minutes, or until a wooden skewer inserted into the center of the cake comes out clean. Invert the hot cake onto a large platter and scrape the remaining topping off the skillet and spoon it onto the cake. Cut the cake into wedges and serve warm.

LANA BOLDT'S PEAR KUCHEN

An Oregon native, Lana Boldt got this recipe from her German grandmother. The flavor of the traditional German cake is rich, the cake is golden and gorgeous, and the aroma is mouthwatering. You can substitute stone fruits: peaches, plums, cherries, apricots, or nectarines.

MAKES ONE 11-INCH ROUND CAKE; SERVES 8 TO 10

Batter

½ cup (1 stick) butter at room
    temperature
½ cup sugar
3 large eggs
½ teaspoon vanilla extract
½ teaspoon anise extract
Grated zest of 1 lemon
1 cup unbleached all-purpose flour

6 medium ripe Bartlett or Bosc pears,
    cored, peeled, and cut in half
    lengthwise
Juice of 1 lemon
½ teaspoon aniseed
3 tablespoons sugar

PREHEAT THE OVEN to 375°F. Generously butter an 11-inch spring-form pan, then coat it with flour and set it aside.

TO MAKE THE BATTER: Place the butter and sugar in a food processor fitted with the steel blade and process until mixed. Break the eggs in through the feed tube with the motor running, then add the vanilla extract, anise extract, and lemon zest. Open the lid and sprinkle in the flour, scraping down the sides of the bowl with a rubber spatula. Pulse 5 to 6 times to blend. To mix by hand, use a medium bowl and an electric mixer on high speed. Mix the sugar and butter thoroughly, then add the eggs and mix. Add the vanilla extract, anise extract, and lemon zest and mix. Sprinkle the flour over the top, then mix for 2 minutes.

POUR THE BATTER into the prepared pan. Cut the rounded edge off each pear half so it will lie flat. Arrange the halved pears in a spoke pattern in the batter, cut-side up and rounded side down. Place the cut pear pieces along the outside rim of the pan. Sprinkle the pears with lemon juice, aniseed, and sugar. Bake until the kuchen is brown and a toothpick inserted in the center comes out clean, about 40 minutes. Let cool for 30 minutes on a rack, then remove from the pan and serve.

BARTLETT ICE CREAM

In the good old summertime, when the first pears appear, make this ice cream using the pears that don't look quite pretty enough to eat out of hand. Made into ice cream, they're memorable. Start with a cooked custard, add a pear purée, then use your ice cream maker for this old-time treat.

MAKES 1 QUART

2 cups whole milk

2 cups heavy (whipping) cream

1 cinnamon stick

6 Bartlett pears, cored, peeled, and chopped

6 large egg yolks

½ cup sugar, or to taste

2 tablespoons pear eau-de-vie (pear brandy)

COMBINE THE MILK, cream, and cinnamon stick in a medium saucepan. Heat over medium-low heat until small bubbles appear around the edge, then remove, cover, and set aside for 30 to 45 minutes.

MEANWHILE, place the chopped pears in a large saucepan over medium-high heat and cook and stir for about 45 minutes, or until they're reduced to a thick sauce. Let cool, then purée in a food processor, blender, or food mill. Set aside.

BEAT THE EGG YOLKS and sugar until ropy, about 5 minutes, using an electric mixer, a wire whisk, or a food processor fitted with the steel blade. Bring the milk mixture to a simmer and spoon about 1 cup of the hot milk into the eggs. Whisk vigorously, pour the eggs into the milk, and cook over low heat, stirring constantly with a wooden spoon until the mixture is thick enough to coat the back of a spoon, about 5 minutes. Stir the purée into the custard mixture. Cover and refrigerate until completely chilled. (Use an ice-water bath if you're in a hurry.) Stir in the eau-de-vie, add sugar if needed, then freeze in an ice cream maker, following the manufacturer's instructions.

NOTE: Freezing tames flavors. Add more sugar if pears aren't intensely sweet.

PEAR-GINGER SORBET

Serve this for a palate cleanser at your
Thanksgiving dinner between the turkey and the next course.
It's a fantastic fat-free dessert as well.

MAKES 6 SERVINGS

1 cup sugar

2 cups water

Grated zest of 1 lemon

One 1-inch piece vanilla bean,
    crushed

One 1-inch piece cinnamon stick,
    broken into pieces

3 pounds chopped ripe pears of your
    choice, cored, peeled, and
    chopped

3 tablespoons fresh lemon juice

2 tablespoons pear eau-de-vie (pear
    brandy)

Fresh mint sprigs or basil leaves with
    flowers for garnish

MIX THE SUGAR, water, zest, vanilla, and cinnamon stick in a medium saucepan. Bring to a boil and cook for 3 minutes. Add the pears, reduce heat to medium low and simmer until the pears are tender, about 15 to 20 minutes. Remove and discard the vanilla bean and cinnamon stick.

PURÉE THE PEARS in a food processor fitted with the steel blade, a blender, or a food mill, then combine the purée with the lemon juice and eau-de-vie.

POUR THE MIXTURE into ice trays or a 9-inch square cake pan. Freeze just until the mixture is mushy in the center, then turn it into a chilled bowl and beat with an electric mixer or food processor until the mixture is creamy and smooth. Spoon back into the container, lay a piece of plastic wrap directly on the surface, and freeze until firm. Remove from the freezer about 10 minutes before serving time. Spoon into chilled balloon wineglasses and serve with a sprig of mint or a basil leaf with flowers.

ACCOMPANIMENTS

BITTERSWEET COCOA SAUCE
MAKES 1½ CUPS

¾ cup unsweetened Dutch-process
    cocoa
½ cup sugar
¾ cup 2 percent milk
2 tablespoons butter
1 teaspoon vanilla extract
¼ teaspoon ground cinnamon

MIX THE COCOA and sugar in a
small saucepan. Stir in the milk and
add the butter. Heat over medium heat
until boiling, stirring constantly. Reduce heat and simmer until the sauce
is smooth and slightly thickened,
about 10 minutes. Remove from heat
and stir in the vanilla and cinnamon.
Transfer to a clean pint jar with a lid
and refrigerate, covered, for up to 1
month. Reheat for 1 minute in a microwave, or for 5 minutes by setting
the jar in a saucepan of water and
bringing the water to a boil.

HOT FUDGE SAUCE
MAKES ½ CUP

¼ cup heavy (whipping) cream
2 tablespoons milk
½ cup sugar
Two 1-ounce squares unsweetened
    chocolate
2 tablespoons unsalted butter
½ teaspoon almond extract

IN A MEDIUM microwavable bowl,
mix the cream, milk, and sugar. Microwave, uncovered on High (100 percent power) for 2 minutes, stirring
halfway through. Add the chocolate
squares and microwave on High (100
percent power) for 30 seconds. Stir
the melting chocolate into the mixture, then add the butter and almond
extract. Stir to mix.
ALTERNATIVELY, combine ingredients in a double boiler over boiling
water and cook and stir until the sauce
thickens, about 8 to 10 minutes.

CUSTARD SAUCE

MAKES 2 CUPS

1½ cups milk
6 large egg yolks
⅔ cup sugar
1 tablespoon vanilla extract
3 tablespoons butter (optional)
2 tablespoons rum, liqueur, or brandy
(optional)

PLACE THE MILK in a 2-cup glass measure and heat in the microwave on High (100 percent power) for 3 minutes. Meanwhile, in a large microwavable bowl, whisk the egg yolks until foamy. Add the sugar 1 tablespoon at a time and continue whisking for about 2 minutes, or until the mixture is smooth.

USING A WOODEN SPOON, stir the hot milk into the egg mixture, taking care not to foam the sauce. Microwave on Medium-High (70 percent power) for 1 minute. Stir; continue to heat, stirring and checking at 15-second intervals until sauce coats the back of a spoon and forms a light, creamy layer that holds its shape when you draw your finger across it. When you're stirring the sauce, look at it closely — you do not want it to boil, or the egg yolks will curdle; the barely bubbling mixture should thicken around the edges. If you see steam rising, stop the microwave. The sauce will be just hot enough. Remove the sauce from the microwave and beat in the optional butter and rum if desired. (Sometimes I just leave it as it is, the pure vanilla flavor being enough.)

ALTERNATIVELY, make the sauce in the top of a double boiler over boiling water, stirring for about 15 minutes until the sauce coats the back of a spoon as described above.

CUSTARD SAUCE may be covered and stored in the refrigerator for several days and may be served cold or warm. Reheat in the microwave for 30 seconds or so, or in a double boiler for about 5 minutes.

PEAR COULIS

Combine 2 chopped ripe pears, ¼ cup raisins, ½ cup orange marmalade, and 1 tablespoon minced crystallized ginger in a bowl. Makes 1 cup.

COUSCOUS

Bring 1½ cups homemade or canned low-salt chicken broth to a boil in a medium saucepan. Remove from heat. Stir 1 cup couscous into the broth, cover, and let sit for 5 minutes. Fluff with a fork. Makes 2 cups, or about 4 servings.

PERFECT RICE

A RICE COOKER makes perfect rice every time, and you don't even have to use a measure to get it just right—all you need is your knuckle. Pour long-grain rice into the rice cooker pan—1 cup is about right for 4 people. Place your index finger on top of the dry rice. Pour water into the pan just until it reaches your first knuckle, about 1 inch above the level of the rice. Stir in about ½ teaspoon of salt. Cover the pan, turn the cooker on, and within about 15 minutes you'll have perfect rice. If you prefer to measure the water more precisely, the ratio is 1½ to 1. This means that for every 1½ cups of water you will use 1 cup of dry rice. Makes 3 cups cooked rice, or 4 servings.

CALENDAR OF AVAILABILITY

	July	Aug	Sept	Oct	Nov
ANJOU				*	*
BARTLETT	*	*	*	*	*
BOSC			*	*	*
COMICE		*	*	*	*
FORELLE			*	*	*
RED BARTLETT		*	*	*	*
SECKEL		*	*	*	*
WINTER NELIS		*	*	*	*

Dec	Jan	Feb	Mar	Apr	May	June
*	*	*	*	*	*	*
*						
*	*	*	*	*	*	
*	*	*	*			
*	*	*				
*						
*	*	*				
*	*	*	*			

CALENDAR OF AVAILABILITY

PEAR CHARACTERISTICS

Pear Variety	Texture, Flavor	Fresh, Out of Hand, Salads
ANJOU	Sweet; juicy when ripe	Excellent
BARTLETT	Silky; aromatic	Excellent
BOSC	Aromatic, nutty, firm, dense flesh	Very good
CLAPP FAVORITE	Sweet, herbaceous	Very good
COMICE	Buttery, sweet; juicy when ripe	Excellent
DEVOE	Juicy, firm	Good
FORELLE*	Sweet	Very good
PACKHAM	Fine grained, juicy	Very good
RED ANJOU	Sweet; juicy when ripe	Excellent
RED BARTLETT	Silky; aromatic	Excellent
SECKEL*	Particularly sweet; dense flesh	Excellent
WINTER NELIS	Sweet, aromatic	Very good

*Although their flavor and texture make these pears very good for many cooking purposes, they are small in size.

Baking, Poaching	Pies	Muffins, Quick Breads	Canning, Jams, Preserves
Very good	Good	Very good	Fair
Excellent	Excellent	Excellent	Excellent
Excellent	Excellent	Excellent	Very good
Good	Good	Good	Good
Fair	Poor	Good	Poor
Excellent	Excellent	Very good	Good
Good	Good	Good	Good
Excellent	Excellent	Good	Good
Very good	Good	Very Good	Good
Excellent	Excellent	Excellent	Excellent
Good	Good	Very good	Excellent
Good	Good	Very good	Good

INDEX

TABLE OF EQUIVALENTS

*The exact equivalents in the following tables
have been rounded for convenience.*

US/UK	METRIC
oz - ounce	g - gram
lb - pound	kg - kilogram
in - inch	mm - millimeter
ft - foot	cm - centimeter
tbl - tablespoon	ml - milliliter
fl oz - fluid ounce	l - liter
qt - quart	

WEIGHTS

US/UK	Metric
1 oz	30 g
2 oz	60 g
3 oz	90 g
4 oz (¼ lb)	125 g
5 oz (⅓ lb)	155 g
6 oz	185 g
7 oz	220 g
8 oz (½ lb)	250 g
10 oz	315 g
12 oz (¾ lb)	375 g
14 oz	440 g
16 oz (1 lb)	500 g
1½ lb	750 g
2 lb	1 kg
3 lb	1.5 kg

OVEN TEMPERATURES

Fahrenheit	Celsius	Gas
250	120	½
275	140	1
300	150	2
325	160	3
350	180	4
375	190	5
400	200	6
425	220	7
450	230	8
475	240	9
500	260	10

LIQUIDS

US	Metric	UK
2 tb	30 ml	1 FL OZ
¼ cup	60 ml	2 fl oz
⅓ cup	80 ml	3 fl oz
½ cup	125 ml	4 fl oz
⅔ cup	160 m	5 fl oz
¾ cup	180 ml	6 fl oz
1 cup	250 ml	8 fl oz
1½ cups	375 ml	12 fl oz
2 cups	500 ml	16 fl oz
4 cups/1 qt	1·l	32 fl oz